£16
£11-

The Politics of the Human

The human is a central reference point for human rights, humanitarianism and global justice. But who or what is that human? And given its long history of exclusiveness, when so many of those now recognised as human were denied the name, how much confidence can we attach to the term? *The Politics of the Human* works towards a sense of the human that does without substantive accounts of 'humanity' while also avoiding their opposite – the contentless versions that deny important differences such as race, gender and sexuality. Drawing inspiration from Hannah Arendt's anti-foundationalism, Phillips rejects the idea of 'humanness' as grounded in essential characteristics we can be shown to share. She stresses instead the human as claim and commitment, as enactment and politics of equality. In doing so, she engages with a range of contemporary debates on human dignity, humanism and posthumanism, and argues that none of these is necessary to a strong politics of the human.

ANNE PHILLIPS is Graham Wallas Professor of Political Science at the London School of Economics.

THE SEELEY LECTURES

The John Robert Seeley Lectures have been established by the University of Cambridge as a biennial lecture series in social and political studies, sponsored jointly by the Faculty of History and the University Press. The Seeley Lectures provide a unique forum for distinguished scholars of international reputation to address, in an accessible manner, topics of broad interest in social and political studies. Subsequent to their public delivery in Cambridge, the University Press publishes suitably modified versions of each set of lectures. Professor James Tully delivered the inaugural series of Seeley Lectures in 1994 on the theme of *Constitutionalism in an Age of Diversity*.

The Seeley Lectures include

(1) *Strange Multiplicity: Constitutionalism in an Age of Diversity*
JAMES TULLY
ISBN 978 0 521 47694 2 (paperback)
Published 1995

(2) *The Dignity of Legislation*
JEREMY WALDRON
ISBN 978 0 521 65092 2 (hardback) 978 0 521 65883 6 (paperback)
Published 1999

(3) *Women and Human Development: The Capabilities Approach*
MARTHA C. NUSSBAUM
ISBN 978 0 521 66086 0 (hardback) 978 0 521 00385 8 (paperback)
Published 2000

(4) *Value, Respect, and Attachment*
JOSEPH RAZ
ISBN 978 0 521 80180 5 (hardback) 978 0 521 00022 2 (paperback)
Published 2001

(5) *The Rights of Others: Aliens, Residents, and Citizens*
SEYLA BENHABIB
ISBN 978 0 521 83134 5 (hardback) 978 0 521 53860 2 (paperback)
Published 2004

(6) *Laws of Fear: Beyond the Precautionary Principle*
CASS R. SUNSTEIN
ISBN 978 0 521 84823 7 (hardback) 978 0 521 61512 9 (paperback)
Published 2005

(7) *Counter-Democracy: Politics in an Age of Distrust*
PIERRE ROSANVALLON
ISBN 978 0 521 86622 2 (hardback) 978 0 521 71383 2 (paperback)
Published 2008

(8) *On the People's Terms: A Republican Theory and Model of Democracy*
PHILIP PETTIT
ISBN 978 1 107 00511 2 (hardback) 978 0 521 18212 6 (paperback)
Published 2012

(9) *The Politics of the Human*
ANNE PHILLIPS
ISBN 978 1 107 093973 (hardback) 978 1 107 475830 (paperback)
Published 2015

THE POLITICS OF
THE HUMAN

ANNE PHILLIPS

CAMBRIDGE
UNIVERSITY PRESS

CAMBRIDGE
UNIVERSITY PRESS

University Printing House, Cambridge CB2 8BS, United Kingdom

Cambridge University Press is part of the University of Cambridge.

It furthers the University's mission by disseminating knowledge in the pursuit of education, learning, and research at the highest international levels of excellence.

www.cambridge.org
Information on this title: www.cambridge.org/9781107475830

© Anne Phillips 2015

First published 2015

Printed in the United Kingdom by Clays, St Ives plc

A catalogue record for this publication is available from the British Library.

ISBN 978-1107-09397-3 Hardback
ISBN 978-1-107-47583-0 Paperback

CONTENTS

ACKNOWLEDGEMENTS

This book is a revised and expanded version of the four Sir John Seeley lectures I gave at the University of Cambridge in October/November 2013. I am grateful to the Seeley Committee for inviting me, and to John Robertson for guiding me through the process and chairing the sessions. My thinking on the issues benefitted from many acute points raised in the discussions afterwards. I gave versions of the material at LSE, University College London, University of Birmingham, Australian National University, and the Sydney Political Theory Network, and again benefitted greatly from questions and comments. I am especially grateful to John Breuilly, Clare Chambers, Ciaran Driver, Leigh Jenco, Matthew Kramer, Justine Lacroix, Nicola Lacey, Sumi Madhok, and an anonymous reviewer for Cambridge University Press for their suggestions. I was fortunate enough to be invited to spend two months in early 2014 at ANU, courtesy of the Centre for Moral, Social and Political Theory, and this proved an enormously productive period. Finally, my thanks to Liz Friend-Smith, my editor at Cambridge University Press, for all her help.

1

The politics of the human

To think of oneself primarily as a human being is to discount, in some way, the significance of the divisions we otherwise maintain between people. It will be an important part of my argument, however, that it does not mean setting all those divisions aside. I argue that the politics of the human requires us precisely to address the divisions. It is not that one is human *instead* of being male or female, boss or worker, Ashanti or Fante, Christian, Muslim, or Jew, and that we can therefore ignore the salience of those more specific identifiers in order to focus on our shared humanity. The point, rather, is that none of the distinctions and divisions should prevent us from claiming our equality and being accepted as full equals. Where they do – where the other identifiers get in the way of equality – this points to urgent political tasks. Being human is not a matter of imaginatively discounting the significance of the barriers that have been erected between us, but then leaving those barriers in place. It is not the warm feeling one might get when discovering that people unlike us in every conceivable way nonetheless do things in a characteristically human manner. If those people still have power over us or we over them, we are not yet engaging fully with what it means for us both to be human beings. I do not mean by this that it is meaningless or dishonest to talk of us all being human so long as societies fall short of equality in power. If that were my argument, I would have to postpone the use of the term indefinitely, and probably for ever. My concern is with the tricky way in which notions of the human do indeed call on us to discount the significance of the divisions we maintain between us, and the danger that in doing so they encourage us to set those divisions entirely to one side.

'Humanity,' says Costas Douzinas, 'is an invention of modernity.'[1] Depending on where one places the dawn of modernity, this might be regarded as an exaggeration, but certainly when Cicero used the term *humanitas* in the first century BC, he meant a particular course of studies rather than any claims about our shared humanity.[2] The humanism of Renaissance Europe was also associated with a movement of scholars, in this case seeking to broaden the narrow instruction that had become typical of medieval education, rather than with universalistic ideals of human equality. Samuel Moyn notes that 'neither the cosmopolitanism of the Stoics nor the original concept of humanity were remotely similar in their implications to current versions'.[3] For the Greek and Roman philosophers and their later Renaissance admirers, humanity 'typically connoted an ideal of personal educational distinction, not global moral reform, and only in modern times would coinages

---

[1] Costas Douzinas, *Human Rights and Empire: The Political Philosophy of Cosmopolitanism* (New York and London: Routledge, 2007), 51.

[2] Studies promoting 'the kind of cultural values that one would derive from what used to be called a liberal education'. Nicholas Mann, 'The origins of humanism', in Jill Kraye (ed.) *The Cambridge Companion to Renaissance Humanism* (Cambridge University Press, 1996), 1.

[3] Samuel Moyn, *The Last Utopia: Human Rights in History* (Cambridge MA and London: Belknap Press of Harvard, 2010), 15.

like "humane" and "humanitarian" become thinkable'.[4] And while both Christianity and Islam offered a vision of the world in which birth and status were of secondary importance to whether one embraced their religious teachings – which then edges in a roughly egalitarian direction – these operated such profound gender differentiations that one would hesitate to call them universalistic. The modern notion of the human, intrinsically constituted by ideas of equality and claims about rights, is indeed of recent invention.

The human figures today as an important marker in three discourses. It is the central reference point for human rights, which are explicitly attached to us as humans rather than by virtue of our other identifiers, and are often elaborated in terms of what is necessary for a decent human existence. When justified in this way, they depend on some claim about what is distinctively human. Human rights are sometimes dated to the American Declaration of Independence in 1776 and the French Declaration of the Rights of Man and Citizen in 1789, though as the wording of the latter indicates, 'human' was not yet the operative term.[5] It was not until 1948, in the aftermath of the Second World War, that the Universal Declaration of Human Rights put the language of specifically *human* rights at the centre. In Moyn's analysis, it was not until the 1970s

---

[4] Moyn, *The Last Utopia*, 15.

[5] Lynn Hunt argues that 'The equality, universality, and naturalness of rights gained direct political expression for the first time in the American Declaration of Independence of 1776 and the French Declaration of the Rights of Man and Citizen of 1789.' *Inventing Human Rights: A History* (New York and London: WW Norton and Company, 2007), 21.

and 1980s, in the collapse of dreams about communism and the disillusionment with anti-colonial nationalism, that human rights emerged as our *Last Utopia.*[6]

2) The human also provides the inspiration for humanitarianism, a politics that calls on us to support, defend, and sustain more vulnerable others because of our shared humanity. Like human rights, this gestures towards what we have in common, though in humanitarian discourse, the emphasis is on what we (presumed to be the relatively privileged members of relatively wealthy societies) might owe to less favoured humans, with the less favoured then represented as needy recipients rather than actors in their own right. Cosmopolitan projects of global justice – one of the most rapidly expanding fields of contemporary political theory – are in some ways an amalgam of humanitarianism and human rights, and again take the human as their basis and inspiration. In the global justice literature, the rights and agency of vulnerable others are more firmly asserted than is usually the case with humanitarianism, but the argument is still addressed primarily to the relatively privileged. The key questions are where do *our* responsibilities begin and end, and who owes what to whom?

The above already highlights one persistent worry about the part played by the human in political thinking and life. Human is, in one sense, interchangeable with equality. When we invoke the language of the human, we are refusing the distinctions and hierarchies that otherwise divide us. We are asserting our equality, insisting that we are human too.

---

[6] For his critique of Hunt's alternative dating, see Samuel Moyn, 'On the genealogy of morals', *The Nation*, April 16, 2007.

But the message conveyed becomes subtly different when that common humanity is being asserted on our behalf. The task is then framed more as a matter of justice than equality: the justice that those who have and can owe to those who have not and cannot. In both cases, of course, the language is that of our (human) equality. But in the first instance, those who have been denied their equality and rights are employing it to challenge their subordination and exclusion; they are enacting their equality in the very moment of claiming it. In the second, those already securely established in the enjoyment of their equality and rights are reaching out to vulnerable others in the name of a shared humanity. Though this is not the intention, they enact their own power and privilege in the moment of officially denying it.

In all three cases – humanitarianism, human rights, and global justice – what appears as an assertion of our fundamental human equality can shade off into charity or compassion, and what is meant to challenge inequalities of power can end up confirming them. As regards humanitarianism, this is widely recognised and discussed. In the humanitarian world, all human life is said to be of equal value; indeed, it is part of the self-understanding of humanitarianism that it has instituted what Didier Fassin calls 'the equivalence of lives and the equivalence of suffering'.[7] Yet the very practice depends on and reproduces a non-equivalence in power. At a minimum, those untouched by war, poverty, or tragedy are being called upon to transfer some of their relative wealth to those less fortunate,

---

[7] Didier Fassin, *Humanitarian Reason: A Moral History of the Present* (University of California Press, 2012), 233.

and may need to be cajoled into this by actual or vicarious satisfactions.[8] When humanitarianism is ratcheted up to involve military intervention, the willingness of more powerful states to engage in costly initiatives is almost invariably linked to (though not exclusively propelled by) the opportunities they see of promoting their own economic and political interests. This is not so much about making the world more equal or relations more just, but a process that involves sustaining, sometimes increasing, existing inequalities. Even in the best-case scenarios of the humanitarian mission, where people put their commitment to equality on the line with their lives, the inequalities persist. Despite that assertion of the equivalence of human life, humanitarian missions still (and perhaps inevitably) engage in a hierarchy of humanity when they face decisions about whether the danger to their workers has reached a level where they need to close a mission. At that point, they attribute differential weight to their 'own' expatriate volunteers, to the local staff of the missions, and to the populations whose lives they are seeking to save.[9] It is precisely when conditions have become most dangerous, and the local population is even more at risk, that the mission may feel obliged to close.

It is not so surprising that there should be an ambiguous relationship between the human and equality in the world of humanitarianism, which has always been about appealing to those more favoured by fortune to act on behalf of those

---

[8] What Lilie Chouliaraki calls the 'minor gratifications to the self – the new emotionality of the quiz, the confession of our favourite celebrity, the thrill of the rock concert . . . ' Chouliaraki, *The Ironic Spectator: Solidarity in the Age of Post-Humanitarianism* (Cambridge: Polity Press, 2013), 4.

[9] As discussed in Fassin, *Humanitarian Reason*, especially ch. 9.

less privileged. In the emblematic medallion created by Josiah Wedgwood for the Society for the Abolition of the Slave Trade in 1787, the slave appeals to us in the language of human equality – 'Am I Not a Man and a Brother?' – but he does so as a supplicant, from a kneeling position.[10] In human rights and global justice, the emphasis on rights suggests something more straightforwardly egalitarian, allowing us to see the less fortunate as active participants rather than passive recipients, as people claiming what is owed to them rather than waiting on us to help them. Yet here too the addressees are mainly those higher up the hierarchy, and ideas about the human are framed by a justice rather than equality paradigm. Readers may see this as a strange distinction, for justice is clearly related to equality, and in the decades since the publication of John Rawls' *Theory of Justice* the two terms have sometimes seemed interchangeable. Beyond, however, the commitment to impartiality that must be implicit in any notion of justice, the contemporary linking of justice with equality is largely contingent. Rawls argued that justice requires us to distribute all primary goods equally. The point about this is not just that the equality he argued for was then subject to qualifications that undid much of the radicalism: the objection that many critics have made.[11] The point is that equality is here

---

[10] In her gloss on this medal, Joanna Bourke comments that 'The humanitarian is "naturally" superior to the oppressed person or animal on whose behalf she is petitioning . . . sympathy for the sufferer is infused with symbolic violence.' I think this is too critical, but the ambiguity certainly remains. Joanne Bourke, *What It Means to be Human: Reflections from 1791 to the Present* (London, Virago, 2011), 120.

[11] See G.A. Cohen's critique of Rawls on incentives in 'Incentives, inequality and community' in Stephen Darwall (ed.) *Equal Freedom* (Ann Arbor:

proposed as a second stage, as a requirement of the more primary justice, as something required of us *because* of certain facts or arguments, and that failing these facts or arguments would not, presumably, be required. This primary/secondary relationship becomes especially clear in current debates about global justice. All involved agree on the importance of justice; their disagreements centre on what kind of equality justice might require of us, and whether it requires us to extend our understanding and practices of equality to include all humans, or allows us to restrict these more narrowly to fellow citizens. As this indicates, justice may require equality but is not, of itself, about equality.

Why this matters should become clear in the course of this book, but let me anticipate. I argue here for an understanding of human equality as a claim and commitment: not as the outcome of an argument, nor as the effect of sentimental education, nor as something to be established by reference to certain facts about human beings. There is, in my view, little to be gained through disquisitions about the 'essentials' of human nature. The kinds of things humans are and do covers a vast (and often disturbing) range, and our judgements about which of these is essential to our humanity reflect, as much as anything, our preferences about how we like to see ourselves. Theses about human nature therefore play no role in my argument, and I take issue with essentialist accounts. What I mainly object to, however, and most want to argue against, is the idea

University of Michigan Press, 1995), 331–98; and 'Where the action is: on the site of distributive justice', *Philosophy & Public Affairs* 26/1 (1997) 3–30.

that our status as equals might depend on establishing that we share some common essence. People assert, rather than prove, their claims to be regarded as human. They most often assert this, moreover, from a position where their human equality has been denied.

I do not mean, by this, that we only demonstrate our status as equals when we stand up and claim our rights. Most people, most of the time, do not go around insisting that they are human or asserting their equality, and some people – babies in arms, people in a coma – are in no position to say or assert anything. Since I want to contest, moreover, the notion that we might have to 'qualify' for equality by demonstrating that we are human, it would be absurd simply to substitute making a claim as the alternative qualification. The emphasis I place on the human as claim and commitment is not intended as yet another hurdle we must jump in order to get the appropriate recognition. My point, rather, is that being human and equal is a political rather than cognitive matter; and that there is a crucial difference between the assertion of equality by those previously denied it and the implementation of justice by those with the power and authority to do so. How we understand the politics of the human is very much implicated in this. If we think of the human in terms of what those who have and can owe to those who currently have not and cannot, we miss much of what I take to be most radical in the notion. This is the claim, *by those not yet recognised as such*, that they are of fully equal standing. The human, in my argument, is about claiming our equality, and we do not sufficiently recognise this when we talk only in the language of justice. One of my hopes in writing this book is that I can wrest the figure of the human away from the justice paradigm that has so much dominated recent political theory and restate equality as its central concern.

Difference

My other major objective is to challenge the notion of the human as what we have in common when all our contingent characteristics have been stripped away. Historically, the human has been conceptualised in culturally loaded, gender-coded, and strongly normative terms that have then served as a basis for denying significant groups of humans the name. From the debates about whether the South American Indians had souls or pygmies[12] were human to the so-obvious-that-it-hardly-needed-to-be-justified exclusion of women from the rights of man, 'human' has operated to exclude as much as to include. The characteristics deemed essentially human have turned out, again and again, to be modelled on particular groups of humans, and the history of the term has been more marked by hierarchy than equality. The legacy of that history is by no means spent, but there is now enough recognition of the problematic course of pronouncements on the human to produce what looks like its opposite. When the human is invoked today, it is most commonly in order to deny the significance of difference. What matters, we are told, are not contingent and

---

[12] 'Pygmy' is the term used by colonial and pre-colonial explorers, and refers to a number of distinct peoples, including the Twa, Aka, Baka, and Mbuti, living in parts of Central Africa. I have retained the original term for the purposes of this argument.

ultimately unimportant characteristics such as body shape or skin colour or sexual orientation. What matters is that we are all human beings.

This is a powerful ethical ideal. When we are called upon to disregard our differences and recognise the fundamental humanity we share, this is a major advance on notions of the human that defined it in exclusionary and narrowly self-serving terms. It seems to offer the crucial resource against racism, xenophobia, misogyny, ultranationalism – the many hatreds of the 'other' that dwell obsessively on the differences between us – and treat these as incompatible with living peacefully side by side. In my own work on multiculturalism, I have criticised the exaggerations of difference that come into play when people talk of what they conceive as cultural or national or gender difference, and have challenged the reifications of 'culture' that massively overstate these.[13] In doing so, I do not say we should disregard differences, but when I argue that these are often less substantial than is made out, I seem to embrace something close to that ethical ideal. Echoing Paul Gilroy's comment on the 'crushingly obvious, almost banal human sameness'[14] of our lives, and Lila Abu-Lughod's observation that people do not live their lives 'as robots programmed with "cultural" rules, but as people going through life agonizing over decisions, making mistakes, trying to make themselves look good, enduring tragedies and personal losses, enjoying others, and finding

[13] Anne Phillips *Multiculturalism without Culture* (Princeton University Press, 2007); *Gender and Culture* (Cambridge: Polity Press, 2010).
[14] Paul Gilroy *Against Race: Imagining Political Culture Beyond the Color Line* (Cambridge MA: Belknap Press, 2000), 29.

11

moments of happiness',[15] I have insisted on the commonplace similarities that characterise all our lives.

I stand by this argument, but am also troubled by the suggestion that this imposes my own, ethnocentric, understanding of humans and human life, assuming that everyone everywhere is basically the same – and basically like me. I also worry that it potentially reinforces the idea that being different is a problem. If we respond to those who see society as falling apart because there is too much difference by challenging their assumption that people from other countries or continents *are* so different, we seem to accept the basic premise of their argument. If we respond, to the contrary, by agreeing that there are differences but insisting that these are less important than the fundamental humanity we all share, we again seem to accept the basic premise. In both arguments – as in the xenophobic nationalism they seek to counter – difference continues to be represented as a problem. It is just that in the 'progressive' versions, we minimise either their scale or their significance. We set them aside as less important. We focus on the things that really matter, that shared 'human' core.

The separation, however, between abstract core and inessential difference often works to secure existing relations of power. As Iris Marion Young argues in *Justice and the Politics of Difference*, when we call on people to bracket out their particularities, to think beyond their markers of difference or 'merely local' grievances and concerns, we usually end up affirming the

---

[15] Lila Abu-Lughod, 'Writing against culture' in Richard G. Fox (ed.) *Recapturing Anthropology: Working in the Present* (Sante Fe, NM: School of American Research Press, 1991), 137–62: 158.

dominance of the already dominant.[16] It is those on the margins who are most characterised by and preoccupied with difference: women, not men, who go on about gender; those positioned in a racial or ethnic minority who insist on the pertinence of race. If you are already more securely established in the hierarchies of power, it is that much easier to set your particularities aside. They do not thereby vanish, but they require no special attention because they are already more incorporated into what is understood as the human norm. And incorporated is the right term here, for the body plays a key part in this process. Denying the body – proclaiming us all the same 'under the skin' – is a particularly deceptive move, and a poor ally in challenging the privilege of those bodies that currently feel most at home. As Nirmal Puwar has argued, this erasure of the body is least available to those who feel most out of place, to the bodies that have strayed into territory where it is still unusual to find people of their sex, skin colour, sexuality, disability, and so on.[17] 'When a body is emptied of its gender or race, this is a mark of how its position is the privileged norm. Its power emanates from its ability to be seen as just normal, to be without corporeality. Its own gender or race remains invisible: a non-issue.'[18]

I am critical of the obliteration of difference, of the claim that we should look beyond or disregard our differences, and that what matters is the (then necessarily abstract) humanity that unites us. In the politics of the human, we need to

[16] Iris Marion Young, *Justice and the Politics of Difference* (Princeton University Press, 1990).

[17] Nirmal Puwar, *Space Invaders: Race, Gender and Bodies Out of Place* (London: Berg, 2004).

[18] Puwar, *Space Invaders*, 57.

be able to weave a way between annihilating difference and producing it, between denying the significance of something that really matters, and imagining it in some exaggerated projection. In some of its earlier versions, the human was given far too much content: we were offered an overly substantive understanding that either built on the characteristics of certain groups of humans to the exclusion of others, or conjured up an imaginary human that corresponded to no one at all. More common today is a stripped-down, seemingly contentless version that denies the significance of difference. But if the content was suspicious, the lack of content is suspicious too. Though we do indeed need a politics of the human – something that asserts our human equality – this should be neither so loaded with content that it becomes the basis for a hierarchy of human beings, nor so lacking in content that it becomes a disembodied abstraction.

Humanism

The articulation of this need not, and in my view should not, take the form of humanism. Humanism has come under fire from a number of directions in recent decades: for its essentialisms of human nature;[19] its tendency to read the course of human history as the steady progress towards realising the potential implicit in that nature; its misguided confidence in the

[19] In his 'Letter on "Humanism"', Martin Heidegger argued that 'every humanism is either grounded in a metaphysic or is itself to be the ground of one'. Martin Heidegger 'Letter on "Humanism", first published 1946, pp. 239–76 in William McNeill (ed.) Pathmarks (Cambridge University Press, 1998), 265.

powers of science and reason; its celebration of an autonomous, self-determining subject; and so on and on. The criticisms are often overstated, and while this book is not a defence of humanism, it should not be understood as an anti- or posthumanism either. There are things about humanism that are attractive, others that are less so, and as with all 'isms', the good and the bad tend to get rolled up together. Certainly, the writers thought of as humanists in the Renaissance were an appealing enough bunch: they tended to be anti-dogmatic, more tolerant than most of their contemporaries, and often wryly sceptical.[20] In our own time, humanism's reputation for tolerance has taken more of a beating, for the tradition has come to be associated with increasingly strident attacks on religion, and one of the current objections is that humanism presumes too stark a contrast between science and rationality on the one side, religion and faith on the other. John Gray's relentless critiques, for example, revolve around what he sees as humanism's absurd confidence in human agency and quasi-religious faith in science: 'Humanism is a doctrine of salvation – the belief that humankind can take charge of its destiny.'[21] 'Modern humanism is the faith that through science humankind can know the truth – and be free.'[22]

The more typical criticism today homes in on questions of agency: what is said to be humanism's conception of

[20] As illustrated in Alan Ryan's chapter on Humanism in Alan Ryan, *On Politics: A History of Political Thought from Herodotus to the Present* (London: Allen Lane, 2002).

[21] John Gray, *Straw Dogs: Thoughts on Humans and Other Animals* (London: Granta, 2002), 16.

[22] Gray, *Straw Dogs*, 26.

the human as a self-directing, autonomous agent, the actor at the centre of the world. Michel Foucault saw 'Man' as an 'invention of recent date'[23] and humanism as an unstable combination: one that tried to assert the dominance of subjective Man (the free autonomous individual, the source of all meaning) over objective Man (the object of the human sciences, the socially determined object of knowledge), but was endlessly and inevitably thwarted. In his critique of the repressive hypothesis,[24] Foucault also challenged the (broadly humanist) perception of liberation as a matter of freeing oneself from shackles and repressions, and argued that the pursuit of the 'real me', the authentic self, was just a new way of disciplining us into shape. Louis Althusser, meanwhile, was incensed by the 'soft' Marxisms of the 1950s and 1960s that saw capitalism as alienating us from our species-being. He regarded the very notion of a species-being as an absurdity, and repudiated ideas of the 'truly human' in the name of a finally scientific Marxism.[25] He objected, particularly, to the idea that there is an essence of man that provides us with the measure of how badly things have gone wrong and where they 'must' eventually end up: the idea, for example, that humans find their fulfilment in social labour, are alienated from their 'true' being when forced to produce under capitalist conditions, but will eventually be reunited with that true self, under communist conditions of production. Humanism here stands for a teleology that attributes a highly

[23] Michel Foucault, *The Order of Things* (London: Tavistock Publications, 1970), 387.
[24] Especially in Michel Foucault, *History of Sexuality Vol I* (New York: Pantheon Books, 1978).
[25] Louis Althusser, *For Marx* (London: Penguin, 1969) (first published 1966).

normative meaning to human existence, and sees the sweep of history as the process in which that which has been separated is brought back together again. ✸

I too have no time for the essentialisms of human nature or the teleologies of history. I also share some of the reservations about humanism's representation of the free autonomous individual, though the contrast I want to draw between seeing people as agents and seeing them as victims commits me to a stronger emphasis on human agency than appears in some of the current critiques. My own main reservation about humanism is that it may encourage precisely that mindset of overlooking and disregarding difference, encourage us to look beyond or beneath this to the supposedly more important figure of 'the human'. In an essay from the 1940s, Sartre argued that existentialism was a humanism: not the kind of humanism that presumes a universal essence of human nature, or the 'absurd' humanism that 'upholds man as the-end-in-itself and as the supreme value',[26] but a humanism nonetheless in recognising no legislator for man apart from himself. He also, however, wrote a telling critique of the liberal humanist – described in his account as 'the democrat' – who:

> has no eyes for the concrete syntheses with which history confronts him. He recognizes neither Jew, nor Arab, nor Negro, nor bourgeois, nor worker, but only man – man always the same in all times and places . . . to him the individual is only an ensemble of universal traits. It follows

[26] Jean-Paul Sartre 'Existentialism and humanism' (1945) reproduced in Stephen Priest (ed.) *Jean-Paul Sartre: Basic Writings* (London and New York: Routledge, 2001), 25–57: 44.

that his defense of the Jew saves the latter as man and annihilates him as Jew . . . [27]

The contrast Sartre makes between saving someone as abstract man (or human) while annihilating him in his specificity and particularity resonates closely with what will be my own critique.

* * *

I lay out the main lines of my argument in the next two chapters. In Chapter 2, I take issue with substantive accounts of the human, showing how these have worked historically to set particular groups of humans outside the remit of humanity, but also how substantive accounts continue to inform significant strands of contemporary thought. I argue, at the same time, that it is no solution just to move to the opposite: to a stripped-down, seemingly contentless, version of the human that denies the significance of difference. This, in effect, produces an anti-foundationalist account of the human. I have no quarrel with taxonomies of the species that employ physiological characteristics to locate us within an evolutionary line of descent – though I could wish we had settled on something other than 'wise man' (*homo sapiens*) as the name of our species. My target is the more normatively loaded lists of human 'properties' we find in the social and political literature, and the presumption that it is possession of the listed properties that justifies equality. I am, that is, more in sympathy with Plato's description of humans as featherless bipeds than Aristotle's depiction of us as the political animals; and am particularly critical of the notion

[27] Jean-Paul Sartre, *Anti-Semite and Jew: An Exploration of the Etiology of Hate* (New York: Schocken Books, 1948), 55–7.

that our claim to be regarded as equals might be grounded on some set of essentially 'human' characteristics we can be shown to share.

Anti-foundationalism, however, is a large and imprecise category, and in Chapter 3 I engage with two leading theorists, Richard Rorty and Hannah Arendt, both of whom dismiss accounts of human nature but to very different effect. Tracing through my critique of Rorty, and points of similarity with and distance from Arendt, I build up and clarify my case for viewing the politics of the human as an enactment of equality. In Chapter 4, I engage with what I regard as one major challenge to the argument, which comes via the notion of human dignity. The dignity of the human is often claimed as a necessary underpinning to human rights, yet seems to imply precisely the kind of substantive ideal about what it is to be human that I am criticising. I argue that dignity is often just another way of describing what it means to treat others as equals – and that where it is more than this, it edges into territory we would do better to avoid. Finally, in Chapter 5, I return to the relationship between my own arguments and contemporary debates about humanism and posthumanism, and explain why neither of these is necessary to a strong politics of the human.

2

Humans, with content and without

When we speak the language of the human, we engage in a politics of inclusion; yet in offering our definitions of this human, we endorse something that serves to exclude. In any definition, the characteristics named as essential may be highly idealised, sometimes verging on the imaginary, but even when they capture something real the selections made are a matter of history and politics. As Ian Hacking has put it, we 'make up people'.[1] We do not make them up in the sense of conjuring them physically into existence, but when we decide that the crucial distinction is that between man and woman, or human and animal, or heterosexual and gay, we settle on definitions and boundaries that then mark our ways of thinking and living. The idea, for example, that humans divide into two sexes, male and female, is so much taken for granted that we tend to think of it as just a fact of nature – and it does indeed capture something 'real': a difference in our reproductive organs. But differentiating between humans on this basis was never the only possibility. We could, in principle, have decided that the key 'natural' distinction was between the short and the tall. Through much of history, people have claimed variations in skin colour and

---

[1] Ian Hacking, 'Making up people' in Thomas Heller, Morton Sosna, and David E. Wellbery (eds.) *Reconstructing Individualism: Autonomy, Individuality, and the Self in Western Thought* (Stanford University Press, 1986), 222–36.

physiognomy as the key distinctions. So far as male and female is concerned, there may be no great mystery about why reproductive organs came to be viewed as such an important mode of differentiation – societies have to reproduce themselves, after all – but it is worth bearing in mind that this is not just 'natural fact'.[2] We should also bear this in mind when considering the human/non-human distinction.

As Felipe Fernandez-Armesto observes in *So You Think You're Human?*, St Francis of Assisi preached to ravens, St Antony of Padua reportedly administered communion to his horse, and in the – to most of us extraordinary – accounts of the animal trials of fifteenth-, sixteenth-, and seventeenth-century Europe, we glimpse a very different division of the world in which animals seemed to have legal rights 'practically on a par with humans'.[3] In one iconic case in Autun in 1522, rats were summoned to appear before an ecclesiastical court, charged with the wanton destruction of barley crops.[4] (This is one of two hundred or so animal trials that have been identified in Europe, some occurring as recently as the nineteenth century.[5]) The rats of Autun never made it to the court

---

[2] I am offering here a somewhat simplified version of Judith Butler's analysis of the sex/gender distinction, as laid out in her *Gender Trouble* (New York and Oxford: Routledge, 1990).

[3] Felipe Fernandez-Armesto, *So You Think You're Human?* (Oxford University Press, 2009), 52.

[4] Discussed in William Ewald, 'Comparative jurisprudence (1): What was it like to try a rat?' *University of Pennsylvania Law Review* 143/6 (1995), 1889–2149.

[5] Edward Payson Evans, *The Criminal Prosecution and Capital Punishment of Animals* (first published 1906, second edition London: Hesperus Press, 2013).

room, and the ingenious local jurist appointed to defend them, Bartholomew Chassenée, managed to come up with a range of impressive legal arguments justifying their repeated failure to appear. The rats had not been given adequate notice; it had not been made sufficiently clear that the summons applied to all of them; they needed extra time because of the length and difficulty of the journey; finally, they could hardly be expected to answer the summons when doing so would put their very lives in danger, so unless the local cats were restrained, the court could not in fairness expect them to appear. Chassenée argued this last point in terms that would apply to any 'person' unable to present himself with safety and, as Edward Evans notes in his account of the trial, argued it 'as seriously as though it were a question of family feud between Capulet and Montague in Verona or Colonna and Orsini in Rome'.[6] Faced with apparently endless possibilities for legal wrangling, the court lost heart and abandoned the prosecution.

The point about these trials is not that people long ago could not tell the difference between humans and rats, nor that they weirdly assumed that rats and pigs and dogs and grasshoppers (all subject to trial at some point or another) were rational beings capable of the same kind of intentional acts as humans. In his analysis of the Autun case, William Ewald argues that what was going on was a different division of the world, in which humans and animals were regarded equally as creatures of God and the salient distinction was between godly and ungodly: 'godly humans and animals appear on one side of the ledger; ungodly humans and animals on the

---

[6] Evans, *The Criminal Prosecution and Capital Punishment of Animals*, 5.

other'.[7] He goes on to suggest that this way of thinking became increasingly difficult to sustain with the rise of humanism. 'It was the humanist philosophers of the Renaissance who first began to talk, in a new way, about the nobility of being human, and to speak of humans as uniquely created in the image and likeness of God.'[8]

The new significance attached to the human/animal divide did not, as we know, mean that all humans were then included on the same side of the ledger. Being human came to be associated, for example, with rationality and the capacity for normative judgement, but women were widely thought not to exhibit these qualities. In this context, it became possible to set women outside the category of the human, to say that all men have equal rights (because of their common humanity) but mean *only men*. Being human also came to be associated with a specific way of marking one's separation from nature. Again, some humans seemed not to fit this, and these too could be set on the other side of the ledger. In her study of *Race and the Crisis of Humanism*, Kay Anderson notes that 'the distinctive humanity of "the human" [came] to be found in its separateness from nature',[9] and traces how this was fleshed out, from the mid eighteenth century onwards, in an account of human and societal development that saw us passing through supposedly universal stages of hunting, pastorage, cultivation, and commerce. In Anderson's analysis, that 'humanist' understanding of the unity

[7] Ewald, 'What was it like to try a rat?', 1915.

[8] Ewald, 'What was it like to try a rat?', 1915.

[9] Kay Anderson, *Race and the Crisis of Humanism* (London and New York: Routledge, 2007), 11.

and progression of humankind was thrown into crisis by the bewildering behaviour of Australian Aboriginals, who refused to learn settled agriculture and displayed no enthusiasm for separating themselves from nature. At this point, a more optimistic humanism that had viewed all peoples as members of the same human race – that ranked them, certainly, but at least not by *intrinsic* difference, more by contingent assessments of how far they had progressed through the universal stages of development – that more optimistic humanism gave way to the idea of biologically distinct races.

It has been plausibly argued that a growing awareness of our shared vulnerability to suffering and pain played an important role in the flourishing of ideas of human equality in Europe in the mid eighteenth century.[10] Focusing on the body we all share looks a more promising commonality, for however much we may vary in our exercise of reason or desire to separate ourselves from nature, all our bodies are vulnerable to pain. Recognising one's own bodily vulnerability then seems a first step towards recognising the equal vulnerability of others. Or as Judith Butler has put it, 'the recognition of shared precariousness introduces strong normative commitments of equality'.[11] In the arguments I develop in this book, I too represent the body as playing an important role in the development of claims to equality, and much of my objection to contentless

[10] Hunt, *Inventing Human Rights*; Thomas W Laqueur 'Bodies, details and the humanitarian narrative' pp. 176–204 in Lynn Hunt (ed.) *The New Cultural History* (Berkeley LA and London: University of California Press, 1989).

[11] Judith Butler, *Frames of War: When is Life Grievable?* (New York and London: Verso, 2009), 28–9.

understandings of humanity lies in their attempts to erase the body. But even the obviously shared body failed to transcend racial or gender or status divides. In many cases it was simply assumed that there were 'higher' and 'lower' categories of humans, and that the lower kinds did not feel much pain. In *What It Means to Be Human*, Joanna Bourke gives an example from an 1875 defence of vivisection that used presumed differences in pain threshold among humans to justify the ill-treatment of animals: 'What would be torture to one creature is barely felt by the other. Even amongst the lower types of man feeling is less acute, and blows and cuts are treated with indifference by the aboriginal Australian which would lay a European in hospital.'[12] Note again how the Australian Aboriginal figures.

The historical evidence about exclusionary uses of the human is pretty much beyond debate, though it is worth stressing that much of this took the form of denying certain groups of humans the status of *personhood*, rather than failing even to see them as human beings. There was, as Bourke puts it, 'no unambiguous correspondence between physically resembling other humans and being culturally and morally "a person"'.[13] So when women, for example, were declared ineligible to serve on juries in the state of Massachusetts despite legislation stressing the eligibility of 'every person qualified to vote', the state supreme court had no qualms about interpreting person as male person, and wrote that 'no intention to include women can be deduced from the omission of the word "male"'.[14] It would

---

[12] Vivisection tract, 1875, quoted in Bourke, *What It Means to be Human*, 78.
[13] Bourke, *What It Means to be Human*, 127.
[14] Cited in Martha C. Nussbaum, 'Human functioning and social justice: in defense of Aristotleian essentialism', *Political Theory* 20/2 (1992), 227.

have been harder, Martha Nussbaum argues, for the court to make this move with the notion of human being. 'Whatever the differences we encounter, we are rarely in doubt as to when we are dealing with a human being and when we are not.'[15] It was the normative significance of being human that was mostly at stake, not whether you could tell the difference between a rat and a human. This normative status was repeatedly denied to women, Native Americans, African slaves, pygmies, and so on.

Is this still a problem?

We can presumably agree that the history of the human has been one of repeated exclusions. Is this still a problem? People no longer debate whether South American Indians have souls or pygmies are human, and those now working with the concept of the human mostly aim to minimise the substance they attach to the term. It is rare, nowadays, to locate entitlements to the vote or to serve on juries in detailed content-laden claims about the nature of human beings, or to employ that content to deny certain humans the name. There remain significant exceptions, especially as regards gender. In a number of countries, having a *female* nature still disqualifies one from voting or education or particular occupations, or makes one's evidence in legal cases less weighty than that of a man. In many ways, we also continue to operate with understandings of the human that implicitly reference particular kinds of bodies and experience. Women are not, on the whole, now regarded as

[15] Nussbaum, 'Human functioning and social justice', 215.

less than or other than human, but it remains almost impossible for them to function as the generic human.[16] As Catharine MacKinnon has noted, when women and men alike are subjected to violence or torture, this is typically understood as a violation of *human* rights; and unless we are explicitly told that some of the victims are women, we probably imagine them as male.[17] When, however, what happens is seen as more specific to women – rape, perhaps, or domestic violence – this is not so readily understood as a violation of humanity, but is discussed as a violation of *women's* rights. Even today, that is, it is hard for us to conceptualise a woman as the generic human. Since it is hard to conceptualise a generic human without some visual image, it is usually the male body that fills this space.

This is one sense in which little has changed. It is also the case that while most contemporary writing on global justice or human rights now strives to avoid overly substantive versions of 'the human', it is proving hard to abandon entirely the idea that our rights and claims depend on *something* about human nature. The natural law tradition is mostly a thing of the past; many now agree with Jeremy Bentham that natural rights are 'nonsense'; but the idea that there is something inherent in humans that provides the basis for our rights and claims continues to appeal. It is not uncommon to come across definitions of human rights like the following one, taken from Lynn Hunt:

---

[16] See, for example, V. Spike Peterson and Laura Parisi, 'Are women human? It's not an academic question', pp. 132–60 in Tony Evans (ed.) *Human Rights Fifty Years On: A Reappraisal* (Manchester University Press, 1998).

[17] Catharine A. MacKinnon, *Are Women Human? And Other International Dialogues* (Cambridge MA and London: Belknap Press of Harvard, 2007), 180.

'Human rights require three interlocking qualities: rights must be *natural* (inherent in human beings); *equal* (the same for everyone); and *universal* (applicable everywhere).'[18] And while a significant strand of rights theorising rejects all references to nature and represents human rights as entirely political and conventional, there is also an important contemporary line of justification that locates them in personhood and another that locates them in basic human needs.

The first invokes the usual suspects of agency and the capacity to formulate and reflect on a conception of the good, thereby leaving a considerable proportion of the human population – babies, young children, those with severe cognitive disabilities, those in a coma – in a kind of non-rights limbo. Allen Buchanan, for example, explicitly distinguishes between human beings and persons, and argues that it is personhood that confers the rights we loosely term 'human'.[19] The exclusionary line then shifts from human/non-human (all human beings are now recognised as human) to what is said to be the normatively significant sub-division (who has the capacities associated with being a person?). The second, basic needs, approach slides between the nutritional or reproductive needs we share with all animals (which can hardly ground specifically human rights) and more substantive normative conceptions of what it is to be human. When Simon Caney, for example, offers his first tentative list of common needs and

[18] Hunt, *Inventing Human Rights*, 20.
[19] Allen Buchanan, 'Moral status and human enhancement', *Philosophy and Public Affairs* 37/4 (2009), 346–81.

vulnerabilities, these turn out to be ones we share with many non-humans: we suffer, he says, 'from physical pain, require food and water to survive, and are susceptible to disease, sickness and malnutrition'.[20] Left like that, the argument is self-evidently vulnerable to criticism for illegitimately favouring humans over the other animals who share these needs.[21] Caney's common needs are then supplemented by a more substantial account of common goods and ends that draws on Martha Nussbaum's list of the basic capabilities. These range from the relatively uncontroversial 'ability to live a full life' (who or what would not want that?) to having opportunities for friendship, being able to care for other species, being able to play. The features offered are inevitably controversial. Attempts at listing the common features of the human either fail to differentiate in a convincing manner between human and non-human animals, or do so at the cost of proposing characteristics we will endlessly squabble about.

That we disagree is not itself an objection, and since I am not proposing an unbroken continuum between human and non-human, I too draw a line, if only on the very standard basis of the species. I do not, however, see these species features as *justifying* our moral status – and this is not because something else justifies it instead, but because justification of that status is not the issue. Justification is also not the primary issue for most

[20] Simon Caney, *Justice Beyond Borders: A Global Political Theory* (Oxford University Press, 2005), 36.

[21] As is indeed argued in Alasdair Cochrane, 'From human rights to sentient rights', *Critical Review of International Social and Political Philosophy* 16/5 (2013), 655–75.

of those now working on human rights, needs, and capabilities. Contributors range between those (like David Miller[22]) who limit themselves to what they see as the most urgent human needs, and those (like Martha Nussbaum) who make strong claims about what is necessary to a decent human life; but in all cases the work is primarily aimed at convincing citizens or governments of their obligations to uphold certain (minimal or maximal) standards, and is not normally understood as regulating who does or doesn't count as human. In one rare exception to this, Nussbaum acknowledges that strong claims about what makes us truly human do imply strong claims about who is in and who is out. 'It is safe to say that if we imagine a tribe whose members totally lack sense perception or totally lack imagination or totally lack reasoning and thinking, we are not in any of these cases imagining a tribe of human beings, no matter what they look like.'[23] 'Totally lacking sense perception' looks relatively uncontentious (this would seem to rule out all animals), and even the most determined misogynist would hardly say women 'totally lack all thinking'. But 'totally lacking imagination'?

[22] Miller, working within what I have described as a justice paradigm and preoccupied with what justifies the obligations attached to claims about human rights, argues that we need a compelling 'non-sectarian' grounding for rights that can be accepted in liberal and non-liberal societies alike. He finds this in the urgent human needs that set the conditions for a decent life, and is resolutely minimal in his formulation of these. David Miller, *National Responsibility and Global Justice* (Oxford University Press, 2007); Miller, 'Grounding human rights', *Critical Review of International Social and Political Philosophy* 15/4, (2012), 407–27.

[23] Nussbaum, 'Human functioning and social justice', 218.

In *The Inheritors*, William Golding's novel about a tragic encounter between a small group of Neanderthals and a fiercer and more proficient group of *homo sapiens*, imagination is indeed one of the things the Neanderthals have trouble with. Lok, the happy-go-lucky and not-so-smart Neanderthal through whom most of the story is told (towards the end the perspective shifts to that of the victorious 'New People'), has 'pictures in his head', but most of the time cannot work out what these are. Are they memories, plans, wishes? Pictures of things that have happened, are happening, are going to happen? Since the Neanderthals in the story seem able to share one another's pictures, are they some form of telepathic communication? It is the power of Golding's writing that you do see the Neanderthals as human beings, though they do not look much like the 'New People', are not capable of anything approximating *homo sapiens*' powers of planning, and – depending on what we mean by the term – do not seem to have imagination. Significantly, the Neanderthals assume throughout that, different and disturbing as they are, the 'New People' are people like themselves. *Homo sapiens* displays no such generosity of spirit, and by the end of the book the Neanderthals are either captured or killed. I do not at all mean to suggest that Nussbaum would have countenanced this – this would be entirely at odds with the positions she has developed as regards justice to other species – but attaching such substantive characteristics to the human is always going to be problematic. Ruling on who counts as human is never a primary object in contemporary formulations of rights, needs, and capabilities, and we are not any longer in the business of denying groups of humans the name. (We are more in the business, as Alasdair Cochrane notes, of policing the boundaries between human and animal, and ensuring that the latter don't get too many rights.[24]) But insofar as theories depend on substantive claims about human nature, they continue to carry this implication.

In some quarters, indeed, there has been a resurgence of substantive accounts with explicitly exclusionary intent. As people grapple with the ethical implications of revolutions in biotechnology, including the prospect of genetic manipulations that can eliminate some 'human' characteristics and enhance others, there has been a revival of philosophical anthropologies in an attempt to identify what, if anything, marks the boundary of the human. Francis Fukuyama's *Our Posthuman Future* is one notable example of this. Fukuyama insists that we cannot address the challenge of the biotechnological revolution without a notion of human nature, and cannot have meaningful human rights without making judgements about what most matters in that nature.[25] His own definition is both excessively narrow and vacuously wide: 'human nature is the sum of the behavior and characteristics that are typical of the human species, arising from genetic rather than environmental factors'.[26] Why, one might ask, that privileging of genetic

[24] Cochrane, 'From human rights to sentient rights'.

[25] Francis Fukuyama, *Our Posthuman Future: Consequences of the Biotechnology Revolution* (New York: Farrar, Straus and Giroux, 2002). To my mind, Fukuyama mistakes the contemporary resistance to ideas of human nature, attributing it to the (false) belief that humans are infinitely plastic; and mistakes also the resistance to seeing human rights as grounded in human nature, attributing this to a philosophical distaste for arguments that ground an ought in an is. He does not, that is, engage with what I see as the more fundamental problem of exclusion.

[26] Fukuyama, *Our Posthuman Future*, 130.

over environmental factors? Why is something more 'me', more human, if it stems from my genes rather than my environment? Fukuyama later fills in his general definition with human emotion, human reason, and human moral choice, claiming these as the most important of the uniquely human characteristics, and he seems willing to accept the exclusionary implications. Were we, for example, to come across a being who looks like us but is devoid of human emotion, we could, he suggests, quite legitimately double-cross or even kill this Mr Spock-like figure without feeling remorse.[27] The body is here set aside as a relatively unimportant marker of our humanness.

The contentless human

If substantive accounts carry exclusionary implications, the solution, it might seem, is to turn to the other extreme: to strip the human of all particularities, including bodily ones, until it becomes as abstract and generic as possible – a contentless, all-purpose, 'human'. Yet this too has its problems. In his analysis of human rights, Costas Douzinas is unconvinced by the frequent feminist claim (like the one I made earlier in this chapter) that we continue to operate with a notion of the human that references the male body and stereotypically male experience. The problem, in his reading, is almost the opposite: that discourses of humanism, humanity, and human rights work with a notion of species existence in which 'man appears without differentiation or distinction in his nakedness and simplicity, united with all others in an empty nature deprived of

[27] Fukuyama, *Our Posthuman Future*, 169–70.

33

substantive characteristics except for his free will, reason and soul – the universal elements of human essence'.[28] We might want to query (I certainly would) whether 'free will, reason and soul' are quite as empty of substance and specificity as this suggests; and might feel Douzinas' unapologetic use of 'man' and the male pronoun deserves more comment; but I leave this to one side. What he points to is the human as empty cipher, and he illustrates this with a quote from Francis Fukuyama that seems otherwise at odds with his defence of a human essence:

> What the demand for equality of recognition implies is that when we strip all of a person's contingent and accidental characteristics away, there remains some essential human quality underneath that is worthy of a certain minimal kind of respect – call it Factor X. Skin color, looks, social class and wealth, gender, cultural background, and even one's natural talents are all accidents of birth relegated to the class of nonessential characteristics. We make decisions on whom to befriend, whom to marry or do business with, or whom to shun at social events on the basis of these characteristics. But in the political realm we are required to respect people equally on the basis of their possession of Factor X.[29]

This abstraction of the essential human quality from everything that makes us human beings is – to use Douzinas' term – 'bizarre'. It also has the effect of granting us equality *despite* our differences.

[28] Douzinas, *Human Rights and Empire*, 52.
[29] Fukuyama, *Our Posthuman Future*, 149–50.

The injunction to respect people equally is here justified by reference to an abstract core of human capacities, with
all the rest – skin colour, class, gender, culture, talents, and
so on – 'relegated to the class of nonessential characteristics'.
This may sound good, but is not as straightforwardly progressive as it might seem. Consider the practice of blind selection:
shortlisting candidates without knowing their sex or ethnicity,
including that wonderful example of the musicians who audi-
tion for the orchestra from behind a curtain so that the selectors
can no longer tell whether it is a woman or a man who is playing. At the beginning of the 1970s, only about 10 per cent of
musicians in the major US orchestras were female – given that
many women train as musicians, this was an astonishingly low
percentage – but with the introduction of blind auditions, this
rose to roughly 35 per cent by the mid 1990s.[30] (The orchestras
had to do more than just introduce a screen. There was also
a problem that you could tell whether the person audition-
ing was male or female by the sound of the shoes crossing the
stage. The proportion of women selected rose further when a
carpet was added to disguise the sound of the candidates walking across the stage.) Blind selection can be a great technique,
with well-documented and anti-discriminatory effects, but it
is something we need precisely because we cannot yet assume
that selectors will not be unfavourably affected by body shape
or skin colour. It is an indictment of the nature of our prejudices
that we might need blind selection.

[30] One study of this argues that blind selection accounted for about 30 per
cent of that gain. Claudia Goldin and Cecilia Rouse 'Orchestrating
impartiality: the impact of "blind" auditions on female musicians',
American Economic Review 90/4 (2000), 715–41.

In principle, women should *not* have to present themselves as disembodied abstractions – from behind a curtain that
conceals their bodily peculiarities – in order to claim their equal
status in the world. Those with darker skins should *not* have to
insist on us all being the same 'under the skin', should not, that
is, have to present themselves as without skin colour, in order
to be accepted as the equals of those whose skin is lighter. Those
who do not conform to the dominant heterosexuality should
not have to treat their sexuality as a private matter, should not
have to say 'it's none of your business' in order to be confident
of equal treatment. We should not have to pretend away key
aspects of ourselves, ask forbearance in the face of our particularities, or appeal to people to see who and what we are 'beyond'
our gender, skin colour, sexuality, or disability. The idea that we
can separate out some core self – the humanity we share – from
the contingent features that make us who we are represents
those 'contingencies' as of lesser significance, and perhaps even
as things to be slightly ashamed of.

There are three related points here. First, we *are* these
contingencies. We live our lives and engage with those around
us as embodied beings, and the assumptions and expectations
that are attached to our bodily characteristics (assumptions that
vary, of course, from one period of history or one society to
another) profoundly shape our sense of ourselves as well as how
we are perceived by others. We may embrace the assumptions
and expectations and make them our own; we may contest and
subvert them; we may claim to ignore them; but whichever path
we choose, we never emerge unscathed. In trying to imagine
ourselves with different characteristics – what would I be like
had I been born a boy instead of a girl? Had I been an athlete

instead of a scholar? Had I been born two centuries earlier? – we come up against the limits of imagination. We also confront some theoretical incoherence associated with that use of 'I'.

These 'contingencies' are, moreover, what typically drive us to assert our humanness. When we invoke our shared humanity, the self-description does not come out of thin air but is prompted, most commonly, by particularities that have positioned us differently from others in our world. Why would anyone think of claiming to be human – of stating something so blindingly obvious – had there not first been an experience of being denied equal status or respect? And what, other than the particularities, is likely to have been the basis for that denial? When we assert ourselves as humans, it is usually difference, and the exclusions and denials that have become attached to it, that propels us to this point. When we claim our humanity, moreover, we very often do so in the same breath as stressing our specificity: we say 'but we women are human too', 'we Muslims are human too', 'those of us who live on benefits are human too'. We do not claim to be human instead of, or rather than, being a woman, Muslim, poor. We most commonly claim both simultaneously.

Representing differences as contingencies fails to capture what we are as humans and fails to engage with the reasons why we assert our humanity. In suggesting that the differences do not matter, it also signally fails to challenge the many ways in which they do; for if the imaginative setting aside of difference remains no more than an act of imagination, it dissuades us from further analysis of the power differentials that prompt assertions of a common humanity. Much of the resistance to humanism stems from a feeling that it papers over the cracks, obscuring inequalities and brutalities in its invocations of a shared humanity. Rousseau apparently became disenchanted with empty iterations of 'this beautiful word "humanity"', endlessly repeated by what he called 'the least human of people';[31] while Sartre came to think of humanism as profoundly dishonest. In a preface to *The Wretched of the Earth*, published in 1961, he wrote that Fanon's work brings about 'the strip-tease of our humanism. There you can see it, quite naked, and it's not a pretty sight. It was nothing but an ideology of lies, a perfect justification for pillage; its honeyed words, its affectations of sensibility were only alibis for our aggressions.'[32] Telling people whose lives have been devastated by perceived difference that they are human too is at best an empty sentimentality, and at worst Sartre's 'ideology of lies'.

In 1933, after a period in police custody brought home to Hannah Arendt the dangers of remaining in Germany, she left for Paris, where she worked for a number of years with a Jewish welfare organisation. She was interned in 1940, but was able to escape and made her way to the USA, where she lived till her death in 1975. In 1959 she was awarded the Lessing prize and travelled to Hamburg to receive it. This was her first return to Germany since being obliged to leave the country, and she used the occasion to reflect critically on the human and humanity

---

[31] I owe this reference to Hunt, *Inventing Human Rights*, 126–7. The quote is from a letter to Laurent Aymon de Franquières, 15 January 1769, collected in R.A. Leigh (ed.) *Correspondance complète de Jean Jacques Rousseau*, Vol XXVII (Oxford: Voltaire Foundation, 1980).

[32] Jean-Paul Sartre 'Preface' to Frantz Fanon, *The Wretched of the Earth* (London: Penguin, 1967, first published 1961), 21.

and how little these had been able to achieve in those years. As she put it in her acceptance speech, she had for many years 'considered the only adequate reply to the question, Who are you? To be: A Jew. That answer alone took into account the reality of persecution.'[33] It is not that she disparaged humanity or humanness, nor that she always and everywhere regarded herself primarily as a Jew. (And she did not ever regard herself primarily as a woman.) But when Jewishness carried such life and death significance, it was, in her words, evasion simply to insist on a shared humanity.

> (I)n the case of a friendship between a German and a Jew under the conditions of the Third Reich it would scarcely have been a sign of humanness for the friends to have said: Are we not both human beings? It would have been mere evasion of reality and of the world common to both at that time; they would not have been resisting the world as it was. A law that prohibited the intercourse of Jews and Germans could be evaded but could not be defied by people who denied the reality of the distinction. In keeping with a humanness that had not lost the solid ground of reality, a humanness in the midst of the reality of persecution, they would have had to say to each other: A German and a Jew, and friends.[34]

33 Hannah Arendt, 'On humanity in dark times: thoughts about Lessing' (1959) pp. 3–32 in Arendt, *Men in Dark Times* (San Diego and New York: Harcourt Brace, 1983), 17. For a compelling discussion of the speech, see Lisa J. Disch, 'On friendship in "Dark Times"', pp. 285–312 in Bonnie Honig (ed.) *Feminist Interpretations of Hannah Arendt* (Pennsylvania University Press, 1995).

34 Arendt, 'On humanity in dark times', 23.

Saying 'it makes no difference to me' can exhibit great generosity of spirit. But no one should have to rely on generosity to be recognised as an equal, and in the circumstances described by Arendt a willingness to ignore difference denies the violence that makes it matter.

Neither substance nor abstraction

Substantive accounts of the human will not do. When the characteristics attached to the category are spelt out in content-laden detail, they are an obvious hostage to fortune: it is almost inevitable that some groups of humans will fail to meet the criteria, and there is plenty of historical evidence showing that this is precisely what has happened in the past. With any list, there will be some beings we currently regard as non-human who share the characteristics, and some humans who do not. This, indeed, is the classic concern about Peter Singer's work.[35] If we link the entitlement to human rights to characteristics like vulnerability to pain or capacity for conscious planning, the empirical evidence may well lead to the conclusion that some of the great apes qualify for at least some of the so-called human rights. But it may also lead (as it does for Singer and Buchanan) to the conclusion that some humans who currently qualify – day-old infants who have not yet developed consciousness; those in a coma who have lost it – are not entitled. If we use the possession of characteristics to upgrade some of the other primates, we must, in consistency, downgrade some of those currently regarded as human. If, as Jeff

---

[35] Peter Singer, *Animal Liberation* (New York: Avon, 1975).

McMahan argues, 'our fundamental moral reasons not to kill or harm other individuals derive from these individuals' intrinsic properties',[36] then discovering that some animals possess the properties and some humans do not should, indeed, lead us to change our practices: to modify the 'species partiality' that inclines us to rate the claims of radically cognitively impaired human beings over those of cognitively superior animals. If possession of the properties is what counts, that conclusion follows naturally enough.

There have been successive attempts to minimise the properties and reduce the content and deliver a genuinely generic account of what it is to be a human being. Some see Kant's focus on an abstractly understood rational agency as a good exemplar of this – except that his views on both women and 'other races' gesture towards a more substantive hierarchy lurking within that formulation.[37] Others have claimed to identify basic human needs without thereby wandering into dangerously substantive territory, but this is not so easy to do.[38]

---

[36] Jeff McMahan, 'Our fellow creatures', *The Journal of Ethics* 9 (2005) 353–80: 354.

[37] For a relatively supportive account, see Pauline Kleingeld, 'Kant's second thoughts on race', *The Philosophical Quarterly* 57/229 (2007), 573–92.

[38] When David Miller, for example, grounds human rights in 'urgent human needs', he does this so as to find 'non-sectarian' grounding for rights that can be accepted in liberal and non-liberal societies alike. Yet at certain points, even Miller's minimalism fails him. He finds himself unable, for example, to swallow the idea that it would be compatible with a decent human life for women to be denied access to contraception or the right to work outside the home, even though many people in many societies around the world take precisely this view; and then resorts to the claim that it is 'empirically' the case that women need this for a decent

The attempts mostly fail. Either they continue to endorse features derived from the characteristics and experiences of some, but not all, humans. Or they encourage us to view the differences as a problem, and set them aside. The further we go in the second direction – in the direction of the contentless abstraction – the less capable we become of addressing the inequalities that first inspired talk of human rights, humanitarianism, or global justice.

In Chapter 1, I quoted Sartre on the democrat who 'saves the [Jew] as man and annihilates him as Jew'.[39] I take this as pointing to a mismatch between problem and solution, a mismatch between the problem of anti-semitism, which refuses to view the Jew as man, and the liberal humanist solution, which sets the Jewishness to one side and merely insists on his humanity. The anti-semite can only see the Jew as Jew, the humanist can only see him as human, but where, in this, is there space for him being both Jewish *and* human? Or why, to echo a point made in the feminist literature, cannot we be both women *and* human?[40] Why is humanness defined in such

human life. Kieran Oberman argues, with some plausibility, that Miller here falls back on 'sectarian' arguments disguised as factual ones – and inevitably so, he suggests, for if human rights are to have any bite they will never be acceptable to all conceptions of what constitutes a decent human existence or all religious and moral views. Kieran Oberman, 'Beyond sectarianism? On David Miller's theory of human rights', *Res Publica* 19/3 (2013) 275–83.

[39] Sartre, *Anti-Semite and Jew*, 57.

[40] For example, in Mary Wollstonecraft, *A Vindication of The Rights of Woman*, (Boston: Peter Edes, 1792); Carole Pateman, *The Sexual Contract* (Cambridge: Polity Press, 1988); Iris Marion Young, *Justice and the Politics of Difference* (Princeton University Press, 1990).

a way as to make it incompatible with being a woman? Why is it always either modelled on male experience, or turned into something so generic that it is no longer compatible with being either a woman or a man? Why do we have to brush aside as irrelevant our sex, sexuality, religion, or ethnicity in order to be recognised as human beings? And how can it help to do this, given that these are precisely the characteristics that have so often stood in the way of that recognition? When we call on people to disregard their differences and recognise the fundamental humanity they share, this may seem the perfect riposte to those who harbour hatreds of the other, or insist on living only with people they regard as like themselves. Yet as I have argued, it shares the same basic structure with the positions it criticises. Difference continues to be regarded as a problem. Those who invoke our common humanity would clearly repudiate any project that involved *actually eliminating* the differences: moving people around the globe, for example, so as to ensure concentrations of like folk. But in promoting a process of *mental elimination* – setting the differences aside as of lesser significance, erasing the bodies to focus on the deeper 'human' core – they follow a similar logic.

The conclusion I derive from this is that we should jettison the human as a list of properties and stop thinking we need this in order to justify human equality. Whatever candidates we choose as our descriptors, they lead us into questions about who fits and who does not, and may tempt us into treating these as matters of empirical investigation. This may be fair enough when drawing up taxonomies to classify and name species. But when the category 'human' is being employed to justify practices as regards equality or rights, when it takes on a normative significance, the focus on features pushes us in the wrong direction. It is not helpful to think of humanness as a reality that grounds our rights, a set of shared characteristics that we find in some beings but not others, a list of characteristics we can use to work out who gets the rights and who doesn't. Nor is it helpful to make our status as humans depend on not stressing certain of our characteristics, for this is as problematic in its way as making that status depend on having some narrowly defined set. To put this in the language of equality – which is what is really at issue when we talk of the human – the right to be regarded as an equal should not depend on being able to prove one's membership of the category human. Recognising others as equals is a political not cognitive matter. Equality is not an empirical claim, something that could be overturned by new evidence about natural inequalities or new definitions of the species. The very act of claiming to be equal should be enough of a demonstration.

Equality is not something that calls out for justification, and this is only partly because of the hierarchies that lurk behind every version of the human. It also reflects an incoherence in the very idea of justifying or 'proving' equality. The soul, by definition, is not available to empirical evidence. Our supposedly common rationality is often questionable, and not much in evidence in newborn babies. Our vulnerability to pain is shared by non-human animals. But far more to the point, the notion of proving equality is at odds with the claim. In the nineteenth century – that century of biological explanations, to which we owe much of the mythology of racial types – it became commonplace to 'explain' gender differences by reference to the hysteria attendant on having a womb or the stupidity linked to having a tiny brain. One might then imagine the progressive scientist (whom I presume in this instance to be male, for no woman would have had access to the necessary resources or training) embarking on a programme of calculating the average size of women's brains in order to counter the belief that these were smaller than those of men. In the very act of 'disproving' the presumption, 'proving' the equality of the sexes, our generous egalitarian would seem to acknowledge that if the results did not fit with his hypothesis, then regarding the sexes as unequal would be perfectly fair. In seeking to demonstrate that there is no measurable difference between women and men, he would seem to accept the possibility that one sex might indeed be of lesser value. Proving equality is a game it is almost impossible to win, because of the difficulties of what would count as proof. It is also not the kind of game we should be playing. Equality, to echo Hannah Arendt, 'is not given to us';[41] it is not some natural characteristic we are born with, and cannot be either demonstrated or deduced from an underlying human sameness.

My final point, at this stage, is that recognising others as our human equals is not best understood as a process of recognition. Recognise is not really the right term here, for it suggests an uncovering of something previously concealed but already in existence, a finding out rather than creation. Despite, moreover, what we have learnt from Hegel about master and slave alike being involved in the search for recognition, the idea of recognition continues to suggest one group according

---

[41] Hannah Arendt, *The Origins of Totalitarianism* (New York: Schocken Books, 1951), 301.

or granting recognition to another. It works, that is, within a justice paradigm rather than an equality one. The human is not best understood as a matter of uncovering or stripping away, of recognising the similarities that have been concealed by our differences, of delving beneath the specificities of gender, sexuality, religion, ethnicity, or culture to reach the shared human core. What links us (or could/should link us) is a politics of equality that refuses to attach hierarchical significance to difference. Endorsing that politics, moreover, increases rather than reduces the urgency of understanding why particular differences have attracted hierarchical significance, and the determination to change this. Representing our common humanity as *more important* than the differences that drive us to assert it is not the way to achieve this.

3

On not justifying equality: Rorty and Arendt

I have argued for a broadly anti-foundationalist account of the human, but what, precisely, does this mean? The term is closely associated with the work of Richard Rorty, the classic anti-foundationalist, who rejected appeals to human nature and insisted on the mobilising force of empathy over the colder logic of reason as what enables solidarity with others. But anti-foundationalism could also describe the work of Hannah Arendt, who similarly rejected essentialisms of human nature, yet endorsed a strongly normative account of what it is to be human. Arendt was far more suspicious than Rorty of the power of empathy: she likened compassion to being 'stricken with the suffering of someone else as though it were contagious'[1] and saw it as constrained by its focus on individual suffering. Though she thought somewhat more highly of pity, she warned that it has 'as much vested interest in the existence of the unhappy as thirst for power has a vested interest in the existence of the weak'.[2] I use my discussion of these two to further clarify my arguments about the politics of the human. My version of anti-foundationalism leans towards Arendt, though I diverge from her on some important points.

[1] Hannah Arendt, *On Revolution* (New York: Viking Press, 1963), 85.
[2] Arendt, *On Revolution*, 89.

Richard Rorty and the ever expanding circle

Rorty had no truck with the idea of 'proving' essential human characteristics, and is known for his celebration of literature rather than philosophy as what best alerts us to cruelty and promotes solidarity. In his 1993 contribution to the Oxford Amnesty Lectures, he argues that human rights derive their political and moral force not from essential defining features of humanity, but from the everyday stories we tell about others that enable us at last to *see* them. Positioning himself closer to Hume than to Plato, Aquinas or Kant, he suggests that 'to get whites to be nicer to Blacks, males to females, Serbs to Muslims, or straights to gays, to help our species link up into what [Eduardo] Rabossi calls a "planetary community" dominated by a culture of human rights, it is of no use whatever to say, with Kant: Notice that what you have in common, your humanity, is more important than these trivial differences.'[3] Rorty represented himself as agnostic as to whether there *is* anything termed human nature, though in doing so he partially relied on 'what we now know' about the malleability of human nature, which suggests he took up some position on this.[4] But whether there is such a thing or not, the important point is that appealing to it doesn't work. 'Since no useful work seems to be done

[3] Richard Rorty, 'Human rights, rationality, and sentimentality', pp. 111–34 in Stephen Shute and Susan Hurley (eds.) *On Human Rights: The Oxford Amnesty Lectures* (New York: Basic Books, 1993), 125.

[4] As also noted in Jose-Manuel Barreto, 'Rorty and human rights: contingency, emotions and how to defend human rights telling stories', *Utrecht Law Review* 7/2 (2011), 93–112; and Leonard D. G. Ferry, 'Floors without foundations: Ignatieff and Rorty on human rights', *Logos: A Journal of Catholic Thought and Culture* 10/1 (2007), 80–105.

by insisting on a purportedly ahistorical human nature, there probably is no such nature, or at least nothing in that nature that is relevant to our moral choices.'[5] Trying to prove to people that they share a common humanity with those they see as profoundly other is a thankless task. What enables us to see people differently, makes us more tolerant, and ultimately propels us into action on their behalf, are the 'sad and sentimental stories' that alert us to others' suffering and help us see the similarities between their lives and ours. The 'commands of reason' are less effective than 'the suggestions of sentiment' in building a culture of human rights. It is novels, ethnographies, and biographies, rather than philosophy, that make the difference; imaginative re-description rather than argument; our common humanity as evoked rather than uncovered.

Rorty's account is in many ways compelling. I share his scepticism about uncovering or proving our common humanity, and find his arguments additionally attractive in the way they appeal to everyday similarities of the human condition. In Rorty's account, we focus on the mundane and ordinary. We remind ourselves that enemy soldiers also write letters home to their mothers; that illegal immigrants miss their families and friends; that an otherwise disturbingly different woman is 'like me, a mother of small children'.[6] Resemblance plays a key role in this (like Hume, Rorty sees ideas of a common humanity as evoked by resemblance[7]), but it is resemblance at the everyday

---

[5] Rorty, 'Human rights, rationality, and sentimentality', 119.

[6] Richard Rorty, *Contingency, Irony and Solidarity* (Cambridge University Press, 1989), 191.

[7] For Hume, sympathy relies on contiguity, but humanity on resemblance, and because of this is able go beyond the limits of contiguity. See the

rather than metaphysical level. It is the very ordinariness of other people's lives that enables us to cut through prejudices and suspicions and generate the solidarity necessary to human rights, humanitarianism, and projects of global justice.

The emphasis on the power of stories fits well with what has become the dominant strategy of contemporary charities, almost all of which now employ stories of vulnerable individuals to mobilise empathy and encourage donations.[8] The account also resonates with the historical evidence, which shows narratives of suffering playing a considerable role in creating and sustaining notions of a common humanity.[9] It fits with what Thomas Laqueur has argued about the way 'realistic narratives of the lived body'[10] in eighteenth- and nineteenth-century

discussion in Ryan Patrick Hanley, 'David Hume and the "Politics of Humanity"', *Political Theory* 39/2 (2011), 205–33.

[8] See Lilie Chouliaraki, *The Ironic Spectator*. Chouliaraki is herself critical of this trend. She identifies an 'epistemic shift in the communication of solidarity' that moves in a broadly Rortian direction, but describes it as 'the retreat of an other-oriented morality, where doing good to others is about our common humanity and asks nothing back, and the emergence of a self-oriented morality, where doing good to others is about "how I feel" and must, therefore, be rewarded by minor gratifications to the self – the new emotionality of the quiz, the confession of our favourite celebrity, the thrill of the rock concert . . . being only some of the manifestations.' 3–4.

[9] As argued in various contributions to Richard A. Wilson and Richard D. Brown (eds.) *Humanitarianism and Suffering* (Cambridge University Press, 2009).

[10] Thomas W. Laqueur, 'Bodies, details and the humanitarian narrative', 201. See also his later 'Mourning, pity and the work of narrative in the making of "Humanity"', pp. 31–57 in Wilson and Brown (eds.) *Humanitarianism and Suffering*.

medical writings, or the parliamentary enquiries exposing the heat and dirt and claustrophobia of working down coal mines, contributed to the development of humanitarian sensibility. It resonates with what Lynn Hunt has argued about the way eighteenth- and nineteenth-century novels enabled readers to enter into the world of their heroes and heroines and share their feelings of dread, horror, and happiness.[11] In Hunt's argument, the remarkable explosion of human rights talk in mid- to late-eighteenth-century Europe is best understood in the context of this body of imaginative literature that awakened the reader's sensitivity to the tribulations of its fictional characters. 'Equality was not just an abstract concept or a political slogan. It had to be internalized in some fashion.'[12]

All this looks a good deal more plausible than images of us conceding the 'truth' of a shared humanity after being assailed by the force of rational argument. Don't get me wrong: argument matters. Being caught out in logical inconsistency, for example, can be a powerful impetus towards changing one's mind. If we become convinced that our views on gays are incoherent with our other strongly held views on sexuality or love or freedom, we may indeed be 'forced' to agree that one or other of these views is wrong. But the capacity for holding contradictory ideas is often greater than the fear of inconsistency, and humans have developed many innovative ways of dealing with what would otherwise be cognitive dissonance. We have also learnt that our own inability to come up with good counter-arguments is not, of itself, proof that those we are arguing with

[11] Hunt, *Inventing Human Rights.*   [12] Hunt, *Inventing Human Rights*, 27.

are right: it might just be that we are not so good at marshalling arguments or having a bad day. While there *are* those whose minds respond primarily, even exclusively, to the logic of the argument, for most of us arguments involve eliciting sympathy as well as compelling rational assent. We mostly need the narratives and imaginative re-descriptions, which, as Susan James puts it, 'simultaneously engage our emotions and offer us reasons'.[13]

Solidarity as sentimental education has a lot going for it, but how precisely does it enact equality and what place does it leave for difference? One of the worries about the Rortian enlarging of our sensibilities is that it can be highly selective. People do not become sensitised to everyone, and often find it easier to empathise with imagined characters who remain far away. This is something Lacqueur himself stresses. 'It was,' he notes, 'a standard trope of the northern English working-class movement that sensitive people were oblivious to the sufferings of "factory slaves" while they gushed over the evils of black slavery.'[14] The empathy, moreover, sometimes proves little more than a warm feeling. It is one of the oddities in Hunt's argument that she attributes the egalitarianism of the Rights of Man to changes in perception wrought by reading novels – but the novels were almost all about the tribulations of young women from the middle classes, and hardly anyone thought

---

[13] James says this in partial critique of Rorty, whom she regards as setting up an excessively sharp opposition between reason and emotion. Susan James, 'Politics and the progress of sentiments', in Auxier and Hahn (eds.) *The Philosophy of Richard Rorty*, 417.

[14] Laqueur, 'Mourning, pity and the work of narrative in the making of "Humanity"', 33.

that women qualified for these rights.[15] Being alerted to pain and misery does not, it seems, lead automatically to assertions about rights; while being alerted to the pain inflicted on some can destroy the sympathy we might otherwise have felt for those who inflicted the pain. Narratives 'do not come with built-in moral gyroscopes',[16] and heart-rending stories about the brutal treatment wreaked on victims of violence can work simultaneously to annihilate the common humanity of the perpetrators. One might think here of the destruction of the twin towers, and the way empathy for those whose lives were wrecked in this helped anaesthetise many people to the cruelty of torturing people suspected of terrorism. Terrorists – even just those suspected of being terrorists – lost their claim to be regarded as human, because there was so much empathy for the people whose lives they had destroyed. In somewhat similar vein, people suspected of child abuse have been subjected to appalling levels of violence from crowds aroused by heart-rending tales about child victims. Rorty is surely right to stress that, for most of us, the 'commands of reason' are not enough to compel us into action. But the hyper-rationalists have a point when they warn that emotion unchecked by reason can have disastrous results.

Rorty stressed particularity over the abstraction of humanity – 'the word "humanity,"' he says, 'leaves me cold'[17] –

---

[15] I owe this point to Justine Lacroix, personal communication.

[16] Laqueur, 'Mourning, pity and the work of narrative in the making of "Humanity"', 35.

[17] Richard Rorty, 'Response to Norman Geras', in Matthew Festenstein and Simon Thompson (eds.) *Richard Rorty: Critical Dialogues* (Cambridge: Polity Press, 2001), 174.

and in *Contingency, Irony and Solidarity* rather assumes that this goes for all of us. He suggests, for example, that those who risked their lives to help save Jews from the concentration camps probably did not act because they saw them as 'fellow human beings':

> Perhaps some of them did, but surely they would usually, if queried, have used more parochial terms to explain why they were taking risks to protect a given Jew – for example, that this particular Jew was a fellow Milanese, or a fellow Jutlander, or a fellow member of the same union or profession, or a fellow bocce player, or a fellow parent of small children.[18]

Norman Geras has written a compelling critique of this – compelling enough to convince Rorty that he had overstated his case[19] – that uses the accounts of those who did help Jews hide or escape to illuminate the strongly universalist voice in which they explained their actions. Phrases like 'regardless of who they were', 'it did not matter who it was', 'no matter what a person's colour, race, religion or language', 'Jew or German – it made no difference to me': these are the phrases the rescuers repeatedly use. In the words of Eva Anielska, a Polish socialist who helped save many: 'One saw the Jew not as a Jew, but as a persecuted human being, desperately struggling for life and in need of help . . . a persecuted, humiliated human being.'[20]

---

[18] Rorty, *Contingency, Irony and Solidarity*, 190–1.

[19] Rorty, 'Response to Norman Geras', 174.

[20] Quoted in Norman Geras, *Solidarity in the Conversation of Humankind: the Ungroundable Liberalism of Richard Rorty* (London: Verso, 1995), 24.

Reading these accounts, even at second hand through Geras' account of them, leaves one in no doubt that for some people the notion of a common humanity has enormous resonance and power, and that in that moment of history it enabled (some) people to do things for others that being in the same profession or same trade union would never have propelled them to do. This is a challenge to Rorty. It is also, of course, a challenge to my own arguments: to my critique of a common humanity that requires us to 'get beyond' the particularities of gender, race, sexuality, religion, and wrongly represents these more local characteristics as a problem. As regards Rorty, Geras' evidence pretty much scotches the notion that solidarity can always be explained in terms of parochial sympathies. As regards my own arguments, I see it as less decisive, for Geras is describing how the rescuers, not the rescued, understood the significance of difference. Saying that the differences did not matter – 'Jew or German – it made no difference to me' – clearly had powerful resonance for those extending their help and support, and in many cases echoed a religious or ethical code they had learnt from their parents. It is less plausible, however, that it would have been meaningful to those who had been denied their equality, citizenship, security, and potentially lives *because of that difference*. Nothing of what the rescuers did was easy; they all put their lives at risk. But it remains the case that difference did not carry the same burden for them. It was easier for them to put difference aside than for those they were helping to do so.

Perspective matters; and this is part of what limits Rorty's account. Solidarity takes on different shapes whether considered from the perspective of the relatively secure, now imaginatively engaging with the other, or from the perspective of that other. In Rorty's writings, the emphasis is almost always on the relatively secure. The task to which he addresses himself is how to 'extend our sense of "we" to people whom we have previously thought of as "they"',[21] with that 'we' often filled in as 'we liberals' or 'we bourgeois liberals'. The image is very much that of the strong gradually extending their circle of acquaintance to include more of the weak. Indeed, he puts it precisely in these terms when giving an abbreviated account of the progress of moral sentiments:

> technological changes produced changes in socio-economic conditions, and the latter made it possible for more and more people to become literate, and to have enough surplus time and energy to read books, magazines, and newspapers. *The strong found themselves reading about the weak (the slaves, the poor, the women).* [My emphasis] Their imaginations were enlarged and moral progress ensued.[22]

When the strong come to see the weak as sufficiently 'like themselves' to enlist their sympathies, they may well act to improve conditions: donate to charities, campaign against slavery, vote for parties that promise to increase the budget for foreign aid. Nothing, however, necessarily propels them to analyse the circumstances that produced the inequality and brought about that 'weakness'. As Chouliaraki has argued, solidarity as sentimental education can become 'a matter of training the soul

---

[21] Rorty, *Contingency, Irony and Solidarity*, 192.
[22] Richard Rorty, 'Reply to Susan James', in Auxier and Hahn (eds.) *The Philosophy of Richard Rorty*, 430.

rather than a matter of understanding the causes of suffering and debating our responses to it'.[23] The stories may move us, enlarge our imagination, and enable us to see multiple similarities across difference; but the similarity is in many ways misleading and can obscure the necessity for change.

When rich people, for example, notice that – 'like themselves' – those living on welfare benefits love their children, have aspirations, experience humiliation and pain, this may remain a surprised recognition of the common humanity that peers through all the different ways of talking, eating, dressing, and generally living our lives. But the rich and the poor are not the same. As Hemingway reputedly said, in response to what he considered Scott Fitzgerald's romanticisation: 'The rich *are* different from us. They have more money.' When white secular Britons notice that the young Muslim girls in headscarves are – 'like themselves' – wearing lipstick and tight jeans, this may go no further than the comforting re-assurance that we are, after all, much the same. But those girls still face the challenge of living in a society that is hostile to overt displays of religion, and especially overt displays of Islam, and living in families that may limit their freedom of dress – a challenge not equivalently experienced by their white secular counterparts. In these and related cases, the initial assumption of difference was not just misperception. It reflected a genuine difference (an inequality) in respect of resources or status or security or power. If the subsequent discovery that the other is, after all, 'like us' leads us to ignore these inequalities, it lulls us into a state of complacency

[23] Chouliaraki, *The Ironic Spectator*, 182.

about our own place in a world characterised by unequal power relations. Seeing similarities *is* an important part of human solidarity, and I do not understate this. But the similarities do not obliterate the differential power. Acknowledging the everyday similarity of people's lives should not divert us from this.

On this point, I see little to choose between Rorty and more abstract assertions of our common humanity, for both can distract us from the analysis of power relations. The recognition that others are, after all, like oneself, can reduce stereotypes, increase toleration, and make us care more about another's suffering. In caring more, we may make donations to Amnesty International or Médecins San Frontières, petition our governments to increase the foreign aid budget and adopt a more ethical foreign policy, even decide to work for an international human rights body or humanitarian organisation. These are good outcomes, but they do not necessarily get to grips with the specificities of what created the suffering. They will often be palliative rather than life-changing, and remain within the framework of what those who have and can do for those who have not and cannot. Rorty's ever expanding circle of acquaintances promises a solidarity inspired by likeness, but the practice comes closer to compassion or charity. This is not especially egalitarian.

Arendt and the abstract nakedness of being nothing but human

Like Rorty, Arendt had no time for pronouncements on the nature of the human. She talked of the human condition rather than human nature, and stressed this condition as one of both uniqueness and plurality. 'Plurality,' she writes, 'is the condition of human action because we are all the same, that is, human, in such a way that nobody is ever the same as anyone else who ever lived, lives or will live.'[24] In her much quoted phrase, 'men, not Man, live on the earth and inhabit the world'.[25]

As critics have noted, she nonetheless seems to operate with a highly normative account of what it is to be human that lays her open to the kinds of criticism made in the last chapter. Arendt rejected ideas of a knowable or essential human nature – she was profoundly opposed, indeed, to any arguments from nature – but this was not because she viewed these as useless exercises in metaphysics (the Rortian reasons), nor because they introduced substantive criteria that later became a basis for exclusion. Her opposition was closely bound up with what for her was the central problem of the twentieth century, which was the failure of political responsibility. Arendt was preoccupied, in Margaret Canovan's words, with the 'uniquely modern combination of determinism and hubris'[26] that she saw as characterising not only totalitarianism but much of twentieth-century thought and life: the surrender to supposedly irresistible forces of 'nature' combined with the belief that one can do anything. Attributing power to 'nature', thinking of history as progressing with an unstoppable force, regarding humans as determined by biological imperative: these were all anathema to her. They were alibis, in a kind of Sartrean 'bad faith', that relieve us of

---

[24] Arendt, *The Human Condition*, 8.
[25] Arendt, *The Human Condition*, 7.
[26] Margaret Canovan, *Hannah Arendt: A Reinterpretation of Her Political Thought* (Cambridge University Press, 1992), 12.

the responsibility for thinking and acting for ourselves. Saying that something is natural then carried little weight for Arendt. If to be human meant anything, it meant *not* being at the mercy of nature, being *un*natural, engaging in the artifice of politics, assuming political responsibility.

In her writings on the human, she therefore simultaneously refuses any idea of an essential human nature whilst still endorsing a notion of what it is to be fully human. As Andrew Schaap puts it, 'although she eschews any notion of human nature, Arendt nonetheless presumes a particular conception of human flourishing that is associated with the existential achievements of public appearance'.[27] So when she describes plurality as the condition of human action, she is not just saying we are all different and unique. Arendt understood action in a very specific way, differentiating it from labour (which she understood as the ceaseless round of producing what is immediately consumed) and work (the higher activity of producing things that can be put to use). Action, higher again than work, is the process in which we 'insert ourselves into the human world',[28] disclose ourselves to others, risk ourselves with others, and bring something new into existence. In her account, the human condition requires all three, but it is pretty clear that she 'affirmed the existential superiority of action over labor and work'.[29] Her repudiation of a human nature cannot then be read

[27] Andrew Schaap, 'Enacting the right to have rights: Jacques Rancière's critique of Hannah Arendt', *European Journal of Political Theory* 10/1 (2011), 22–45: 24.

[28] Arendt, *The Human Condition*, 176.

[29] Mary Dietz, 'Arendt and the Holocaust', pp. 86–109 in Dana Villa (ed.) *The Cambridge Companion to Hannah Arendt* (Cambridge University

as repudiating all substantive accounts of what it means to be human. To the contrary, she represents us as only really human to the extent that we are *not* natural beings. If the only thing we ever did, for example, was labour, if we spent our entire life dealing with the daily necessities of reproducing ourselves, we would not be distinguishing ourselves from animals in any significant way. She makes the point, moreover, that humans can manage perfectly well without either labour or work – this, after all, is precisely what exploiters do. But without action, without that insertion into the world, we lose what makes us human. 'Men can very well live without laboring, they can force others to labor for them, and they can very well decide to use and enjoy the world of things without themselves adding a single useful object to it; the life of an exploiter or slaveholder and the life of a parasite may be unjust, but they certainly are human. A life without speech and without action, on the other hand . . . is literally dead to the world; it has ceased to be a human life because it is no longer lived among men.'[30]

This is a strongly normative version of what it is to be human. In her account of imperialism, Arendt then seems to do precisely what Kay Anderson identifies in her analysis of race and humanism: fails to see the humanity in people whose ways of living and producing do not fit her conception

---

Press, 2000), 99. Dietz argues that Arendt does not claim action as what makes the better human life, and she represents *The Human Condition* as Arendt trying to conjure up those forms of human action that will best counter the horrific legacy of the Holocaust. Even so, she has to acknowledge that Arendt sees a hierarchy between action, labour, and work.

[30] Arendt, *The Human Condition*, 176.

of the human. Arendt describes the Africans encountered dur-
ing colonial conquest as appearing as '"natural" human beings
who lacked the specifically human character',[31] and the way she
writes her account has suggested to some commentators that
she shared this inability to perceive the Africans as human.[32] It
is not that she justified what she clearly considered the barbarity
of imperialism; its violence, exploitation and murder. But 'natural human' was almost an oxymoron to her. 'Man's "nature"
is only "human" insofar as it opens up to man the possibility of
becoming something highly unnatural, that is, a man.'[33] This
makes it sound as if some humans are not yet fully so.

I do not share her view of the human condition, but
what I still find illuminating in her critique of 'nature' and
'natural man' is the way it reverses the standard relationship
between being human and being equal. It is not, in her account,
that we are human, can 'prove' this by reference to our souls
or rationality or capacity for 'action', and should *therefore* be

[31] Hannah Arendt, *The Origins of Totalitarianism* (New York: Schocken
Books, 1951), 192.

[32] For a reading of these passages as ethnocentric, see Shira Dossa, 'Human
status and politics: Hannah Arendt on the Holocaust', *Canadian Journal
of Political Science* 13/2 (1980), 309–23. For a more sympathetic reading,
see Dan Stone, 'The Holocaust and "The Human"', pp. 232–49 in Richard
H. King and Dan Stone (eds.) *Hannah Arendt and the Uses of History:
Imperialism, Nation, Race and Genocide* (New York and Oxford:
Berghahn Books, 2007).

[33] Arendt, *Origins of Totalitarianism*, 455. In Canovan's gloss on this: 'being
properly human means being to some degree *un*natural: setting human
limits to natural processes; creating lasting structures to house human
life; laying down laws and endowing one another with rights that are
"human" but not "natural".' Canovan, *Hannah Arendt*, 25.

deemed equal. Rather, we become equals, make ourselves equals, through our actions and decisions. 'We are not born equal, we become equal *as members of a group* [my emphasis] on the strength of our decision to guarantee ourselves mutually equal rights.'[34] We do not, that is, move from claims about our human properties to justifications of our equality. Indeed, in her sober reading of twentieth-century Europe, if we have not yet established the equality, the being human part is of little use.[35] In the *Origins of Totalitarianism*, written under the shadow of the Nazi death camps, Arendt wrote of the 'ironical, bitter and belated confirmation of the famous arguments with which Edmund Burke opposed the French Revolution's "Declaration of the Rights of Man"'.[36] In his critique of the French revolution, Edmund Burke counter-posed what he saw as the meaningless

---

[34] Arendt, *Origins of Totalitarianism*, 301. Arendt then agrees with Jeff McMahan that mere membership of a species does not confer moral status. But where McMahan ("Our Fellow Creatures") goes from this to the claim that it is the properties of the individual that confer moral status (so some animals qualify, some humans do not), Arendt argues that 'we' confer moral status, through the politics of establishing ourselves as equals.

[35] Etienne Balibar interprets her, even more radically, as saying that 'apart from the institution of the community . . . *there simply are no humans*'. Balibar, '(De)Constructing the human as human institution: a reflection on the coherence of Hannah Arendt's practical philosophy', *Social Research* 74/3 (2007) 727–38: 733. I see this as a possible reading, though it does not fit with what she also argues about the 'one human right' to membership in a political community. See Christopher Menke, 'The "Aporias of Human Rights" and the "One Human Right": regarding the coherence of Hannah Arendt's argument', *Social Research* 74/3 (2007), 737–62.

[36] Arendt, *Origins of Totalitarianism*, 299.

metaphysics of 'the rights of man' to the historically specific (and genuinely useful) 'rights of Englishmen', and anticipated Jeremy Bentham in considering the former an empty abstraction. In the historical moment of the mid twentieth century, Arendt agreed. As she put it,

> The survivors of the extermination camps, the inmates of concentration and internment camps, and even the comparatively happy stateless people could see without Burke's arguments that the abstract nakedness of being nothing but human was their greatest danger.[37]

'The world found nothing sacred in the abstract nakedness of being human.'[38] When people had reached the point where they had nothing but their *human* rights to cling to, when they had no state willing to recognise them as its citizens, no political authority willing to assume responsibility for their protection or security, they were pretty much doomed. Lacking membership of a political community, they did not even have 'the right to have rights',[39] for this right went with being English, German, Spanish, not with being human. It depended, in her analysis, on living 'in a framework where one is judged by one's actions and opinions', and was then equivalent to the 'right to belong to some kind of organised community'.[40] In

---

[37] Arendt, *Origins of Totalitarianism*, 300.

[38] Arendt, *Origins of Totalitarianism*, 299.

[39] Arendt, *Origins of Totalitarianism*, 296.

[40] The full quote is as follows: 'We became aware of the existence of a right to have rights (and that means to live in a framework where one is judged by one's actions and opinions) and a right to belong to some kind of organized community, only when millions of people emerged who had

twentieth-century Europe that organised community was the nation state. If you did not belong to one of these – if you were a stateless person, or like the Jews in Germany, had been stripped of your citizenship rights[41] – then even the right to have rights came into question. Arendt (on this point, like Rorty) had little confidence in appeals to a common humanity as enabling us to see displaced persons, refugees, or stateless people as rights-holders.

Europe in the 1930s and 1940s provided grim evidence for her view, and in our own time the limited power of human rights or common humanity continues to resonate. If you were a refugee in contemporary Britain, surviving on less than £5 a day, facing the institutionalised suspicion of the UK Border Agency, living in fear of being returned to the country where they tried to kill you, Hannah Arendt's phrase about 'the abstract nakedness of being nothing but human' would surely ring true.[42] Her opposition between the 'merely' human and the citizen casts light on the dangers of being merely human and the way, moreover, that those without statehood can come to be perceived principally in terms of an animal nature, so not only as different from the rest but also as threatening and

lost and could not regain these rights because of the new global political situation.' *Origins of Totalitarianism*, 296–7.

[41] Arendt argues that the Nazis were careful to deprive the Jews of their status as German citizens before embarking on their extermination. *Origins of Totalitarianism*, 296.

[42] Justine Lacroix has reminded me that refugees are not stateless: they are citizens trying to escape their current citizenship, and living in fear of being returned to the dubious 'protection' of their state. The increasing use of Arendt's writings about statelessness to analyse the current situation of refugees is then somewhat odd.

disruptive. This is a compelling idea, later taken up by Giorgio Agamben in his notion of 'bare' life and the way the human body can become so separated from its political status that it can be experimented on at will.[43]

The contrast between the merely human and the citizen also helps clarify why the humanitarian impulse, which recognises the other as human, and as needy and vulnerable in that shared humanity, may nonetheless fail to translate into treating the other as having the same normative weight as oneself. 'It seems,' says Arendt in her account of the disasters of twentieth-century Europe, 'that a man who is nothing but a man has lost the very qualities which make it possible for other people to treat him as a fellow-man.'[44] He becomes 'mere existence', and though mere existence, in her account, includes 'the shape of our bodies and the talents of our minds', these are personal qualities given to us by the mysteries of birth and 'can be adequately dealt with only by the unpredictable hazards of friendship and sympathy, or by the great and incalculable grace of love...'.[45] One might, in Rortian fashion, come to sympathise with these 'mere existents'; one might even come to love them; but neither of these connections makes them co-members of the society. The 'imploring eyes'[46] of the refugees or the victims of a humanitarian emergency may urge us to give aid and protection, but we can respond to that appeal without acknowledging them as actors in their own right. Indeed, the

---

[43] Giorgio Agamben, *Homo Sacer: Sovereign Power and Bare Life* (Stanford University Press, 1995), 159.

[44] Arendt, *Origins of Totalitarianism*, 300.

[45] Arendt, *Origins of Totalitarianism*, 301.   [46] Agamben, *Homo Sacer*, 133.

needier they are, the less likely it is that we will regard them as equals. As Mark Franke puts it, 'that the displaced person may be genuinely understood by the citizen as also human – even as a citizen of humanity – does not bring the citizen any closer to responding equally to the rights claims of others... The principle of humanitarianism invites only humanity. Humanity is insufficient for membership in the political community of the citizen.'[47] Citizenship confers equality; humanness falls short.

Some have then taken Arendt as arguing that human rights are just empty words outside the framework of the nation state.[48] The more plausible reading, in my view, is that human rights had been *made* empty words by the relentless focus on the nation state as the only conceivable form of political community. In her analysis of post-1918 Europe, the great powers set out to 'solve' the problems that had led to the outbreak of World War One by establishing a new world of nation states. Given the poor fit, however, between the people and the new borders, the arrangements had to be supplemented by a variety of Minority Treaties providing special protections for what could be as much as 30 to 50 per cent of the population. In Arendt's analysis, neither the great powers nor the governments

[47] Mark F. N. Franke, 'The unbearable rightfulness of being human: citizenship, displacement, and the right not to have rights', *Citizenship Studies* 15/1 (2011), 39–45: 46.

[48] See Justine Lacroix, 'The "right to have rights" in French political philosophy: conceptualising a cosmopolitan citizenship with Arendt', forthcoming *Constellations*, for the reception of Arendt in France, and the way many French intellectuals read her arguments in *Origins of Totalitarianism* as a straightforward confirmation of Burke's critique.

of the newly created states were seriously committed to the protection of these minorities: 'the representatives of the great nations knew only too well that minorities within nation-states must sooner or later be either assimilated or liquidated'.[49] The new map of Europe resulted, moreover, in a huge rise in the number of stateless peoples, either peoples who resisted relocation to what they were told was their new 'nation', or peoples later deprived of their nationality when 'their' state deemed them in the wrong place. The result was many millions of stateless peoples and 'nationally frustrated peoples',[50] all of whom clung to what they deemed the premise of the post-war settlement: that the only way to assert your rights was by claiming to be a nation, becoming a nation state. State and nation had been made synonymous; shared nationality had become the only route to freedom or security; 'the nation had conquered the state'.[51]

Arendt was not claiming an inherent connection between human rights and nation states, but tracing the disastrous history of twentieth-century Europe that had made them so closely intertwined. This provides us with an argument about rights and equality that is independent of the nature, properties, and qualities of humans, but also does not depend on the states based on shared nationality that came to dominate the twentieth century. It is true that Arendt saw rights and equality as depending on *some kind* of political community, and insofar as her arguments draw on binaries of nature and artifice, private

[49] Arendt, *Origins of Totalitarianism*, 273.
[50] Arendt, *Origins of Totalitarianism*, 272.
[51] Arendt, *Origins of Totalitarianism*, 275.

and public, 'mere existence' and political action, and express an ontology of human flourishing that privileges engagement in public life, they become (to me) that much less compelling. Like Seyla Benhabib, in her more optimistic rendering of 'the right to have rights', I do not think our claims to equality are necessarily bounded by membership of specific political communities;[52] and while I share Arendt's concerns about the decline of political responsibility, I do not see the political community as the only context in which that responsibility can be exercised. What I take from her, nonetheless, is an account of equality as something we *establish* when we treat one another as equal. Equality is not something we need to justify by reference to a shared humanity. To push this further than Arendt herself intended, it is something we bring into existence at the moment we claim it. It is not that we 'recognise' a pre-existing equality or pre-existing humanity: identify something that was always there but had escaped our attention while we were still at the mercy of false ideas about some being born to rule and others having a slavish nature. We are not equal *because* of certain facts about ourselves, *because* we have a soul, *because* we are rational agents, *because* we are vulnerable to pain. Though we may, and often do, articulate our claims in one or other of these languages, equality is something we assert and to which we commit ourselves rather than something we find out. There is no argumentative structure here, of the form, 'I am X therefore Y'.

---

52 Benhabib argues that these rights *are* now potentially available beyond the nation state, in the international regimes that protect the rights of refugees or rights of asylum seekers. Seyla Benhabib, *The Rights of Others: Aliens, Residents and Citizens* (Cambridge University Press, 2004) especially ch. 2.

There is simply no space between the moment of asserting one's humanity and the moment of asserting one's equality.

What kind of equality?

In Arendt's version of this, the equality we bring into existence is and should be exclusively political. Here, again, I part company with her. I have argued that the claim to be regarded as human should not be understood as obliterating the significance of difference, and that when our humanness is made to depend on overlooking or minimising the differences between us, this has the effect of diverting us from the challenges posed by inequality. If we dismiss rather than dwell on our differences, we become less able to identify the ones that reflect inequalities. We encourage ourselves to think that the requirements of equality are adequately met by setting those differences aside.

Though Arendt insisted on our plurality, our difference not sameness, she also seems to argue for precisely this setting of (certain kinds of) difference aside. The equality we bring into existence is, in her argument, a political one, and not to be confused with matters of social and economic equality. She regarded preoccupation with the social and economic as highly dangerous, likely to deform and even destroy politics.[53] When people focus on social problems like poverty or

---

[53] For an excellent discussion of this, see Hanna Fenichel Pitkin, *The Attack of the Blob: Hannah Arendt's Concept of the Social* (University of Chicago Press, 1998).

unemployment they come to regard politics in instrumental terms, as a mechanism for solving social problems or generating economic growth. Instead of experiencing politics as the exercise of public freedom (a very Arendtian notion), they may come to regard political participation more as a burden than anything else. The subsequent denial of political responsibility – the opting out of politics – played a large part, in her view, in the rise of twentieth-century totalitarianism. For Arendt, the equality that is central to the notion of the human is 'an equality of unequals who stand in need of being "equalized" in certain respects for certain purposes',[54] 'a working principle of a political organization in which otherwise unequal people have equal rights'.[55] There is no suggestion in this that the 'unequals' need to be equalised in more than the political sense. Indeed, she saw it as a 'perversion' (her word) of equality to transform it into a social concept: to think of it either as describing how people actually and already are (the naturalistic fallacy); or to take it as the object of politics to make them socially and economically equal.

The limits Arendt set were in many ways self-defeating. In her famous 'Reflections on Little Rock', her critique of the forced desegregation of American schools, she argued that social discrimination was entirely compatible with political equality: that if people chose to holiday, for example, in resorts that specialised only in their own kind, this was not at odds with political equality; and if parents chose to educate their children

---

[54] Arendt, *The Human Condition*, 215.
[55] Arendt, *Origins of Totalitarianism*, 54.

in schools where they would associate with particular kinds of children, this too was not at odds with political equality. On matters such as the equal right to vote, the equal right to sit where one chooses on public transport, or the equal right to marry whom one wishes (at this point, some US states still had laws against so-called miscegenation), there should be no compromise. Nor, indeed, should there be legislation that *enforces* the segregation of schools and thereby builds discrimination into the fabric of the law. But 'equality not only has its origin in the body politic; its validity is clearly restricted to the political realm. Only there are we equals.'[56]

Even in her own terms this seems self-defeating, for the inequalities attendant on segregated schooling contribute, through unequal access to educational and thereby political resources, to important inequalities in the political realm. The line Arendt sought to draw between the political and the social is never as clear as her argument requires, and assertions of political equality will always open up wider debate about the compatibility of this with social and economic inequality. As an account of what people see themselves doing when they enact their equality, Arendt's emphasis on the specifically political is

---

[56] Hannah Arendt, 'Reflections on Little Rock', *Dissent*, Winter (1959), 45–56: 50. For contrasting discussions of her argument, see Jim Bohman, 'The moral costs of political pluralism: the dilemmas of equality and difference in Arendt's "Reflections on Little Rock"', pp. 53–80 in L. May and J. Kohn (eds.) *Hannah Arendt: Twenty Years Later*, (Cambridge: MIT Press, 1996); and Danielle Allen, 'Law's necessary forcefulness: Ralph Ellison and Hannah Arendt on the battle of Little Rock' in A. Smith Laden and D. Owen (eds.) *Multiculturalism and Political Theory* (Cambridge University Press, 2007).

fair enough: when we decide to regard one another as equals we do not thereby commit ourselves to thoroughgoing processes of social and economic equalisation. Mostly we anticipate something more limited: in the case of fellow citizens, an equality in political and civil rights; in the case of fellow humans, that we are equally worthy of respect. Yet once equality gets onto the agenda, the commitment rarely stops there. Unlike Arendt, I welcome this. People start debating the relationship between formal and substantive equality; start exploring social and economic as well as political and civil rights; they ask what kind of equality and equality of what; and, in the process, become more and more ambitious in their egalitarianism.[57] Once equality has entered our vocabulary and ways of thinking it becomes an irritant rubbing away at the complacencies that justify substantive *in*equalities. Even in its most minimal form it therefore opens up and keeps on the agenda a more substantial egalitarianism than Arendt would ever have supported.

Claiming humanness

When we think of claims about human equality and human rights, not as rationally derived from a fundamental sameness, nor as evoked by sad and sentimental stories, but as the expression of a commitment and a claim, we can also

---

[57] I have argued elsewhere that the distinction between equality of opportunity and equality of outcome is not as clear-cut as it is sometimes suggested in political debate. If the outcomes are not equal, this is often a good indication that the opportunities were not either. Anne Phillips, 'Defending equality of outcome', *Journal of Political Philosophy* 12/1 (2004), 1–19.

see that those most lacking equality or rights will often be the ones most active in making this claim. With humanitarianism, but also with global justice, this is not necessarily the case. The less powerful can become the recipients of humanitarian charity without themselves doing very much. If arguments about global justice prove sufficiently convincing, they can even become the beneficiaries of a global redistribution of resources without themselves stirring. But if we seek more than charity, more even than justice, if we want to be accepted as full equals, we usually have to insist: make a fuss, chain ourselves to railings, perhaps even take up arms. In the famous controversy at Valladolid in 1550, Spanish theologians debated whether the American Indians did indeed have souls and could therefore be brought to Christianity, or could be regarded as non-humans and therefore enslaved.[58] Neither option, of course, recognised their right to determine their future for themselves. This was not yet on offer, it was something that would have to be taken. In the later declarations of the Rights of Man there would be no automatic progression from the rights of (white, Christian) man to the rights of all humans. Though some of those white Christian men later played exemplary roles in extending the remit of rights, the crucial impetus came from the excluded.

There are two issues here. One is about what brings about historical change and the role of the displaced or

---

[58] Chandran Kukathas, 'Moral universalism and cultural difference', pp. 581–98 in John Dryzek, Bonnie Honig, Anne Phillips (eds.) *Oxford Handbook of Political Theory* (Oxford University Press, 2006).

subaltern or excluded in this. Was it slave resistance, or the philanthropy of the anti-slavery movement, or the growing profitability of free labour that brought about the end of slavery in the Americas? Was it the rise of the nationalist movements, or political opposition from within the colonising nations, or the greater prospects for profit elsewhere that sounded the death knell of colonialism in Asia and Africa? Was it the militancy of the suffrage campaigns or the gratitude of politicians for women's contribution to the war effort that delivered women the right to vote? These are matters of historical investigation, and while it is unlikely that any major extension of equality could have occurred without pressure from below, this is not something on which to adopt an a priori position. The second issue is whether equality granted by others is the same as equality asserted by oneself. This must also, to some extent, be a matter for historical investigation. But there is an important difference between claiming one's humanity and rights, where the equality is enacted in the moment of claiming it, and being awarded that status and rights because those with the power to grant it have become convinced that this is required by justice.

Equality enacted is more of a jolt to the system than equality granted, and more likely to disrupt the complacencies that attend inequalities.[59] It might be said – against this – that the requirements of justice can be more demanding than

[59] Mark Franke argues that when the 'displaced' act, this potentially reveals to the 'emplaced' – to those more secure in the enjoyment of their status and rights – just how much that enjoyment depended on the supposed contingencies of their class, gender, or race. Instead of thinking 'those

claims to equality: that an argument from justice might impose considerable distributive obligations, for example, or set a high basic minimum for the ways we are treated, while a claim to equality could be satisfied by the merely formal acknowledgement of equal status. On this reading, it is justice that makes the case for a fairer distribution of the world's resources, or fairer access to opportunities, or fairer terms of trade, while equality remains pretty minimal – as Arendt, of course, preferred. We don't just want equality, we might then say, we want justice too. Yet the language of justice continues to direct us to questions of obligation (what do I owe to you?), to matters of treatment (what counts as just treatment?), questions of balance (how should we weigh up competing demands?), and to what we are entitled to receive. We employ arguments from justice when trying to convince those with power to offload some of it. 'It's not fair' is the more typical complaint of children to parents than the other way round; and even in Rawls' original position, where no one is supposed to have power, the exercise is primarily addressed to those who are likely to be the more favoured,

others are human too' and should therefore be recognised as such, they may come to appreciate that their own position was not, after all, a simple function of their humanness, but of their more specific characteristics. Instead of assuming it was prejudice or blindness that prevented previous generations from recognising the equal rights of women, homosexuals, people of colour, the disabled, and so on, they may come to appreciate that their own status and power depended on denying that status and power to others. Coming to recognise this requires more self-reflection and analysis, and a greater challenge to existing power relations, than is involved in simply 'granting' equality. Franke, 'The unbearable rightfulness of being human'.

to get them to think twice about the implications of current arrangements. With equality, it is not so much a matter of convincing those who have the authority to grant it. It is more a matter of making the claim.

Andrew Schaap describes reciprocal recognition of equality as the 'precondition for politics' for Arendt, and contrasts this with Jacques Rancière's understanding of politics as 'the enactment of equality in a situation of inequality'.[60] For Arendt, being established as an equal is what makes you a member of the political community and enables politics to take place: politics (only) happens between equals. For Rancière, most of what goes on in political communities is far from equality – he prefers to call it 'police' rather than 'politics' – and it is only at the moments of 'dissensus', when people *not* regarded as equals, *not* considered qualified to participate, act and speak *as if* they were, that we can begin to talk of politics. I agree that we often – perhaps even typically – enact equality when insisting on it against the odds: when members of the Women's Social and Political Union stand up in a political meeting and unfurl their flag; when Rosa Parks asserts her right to sit where she chooses on the bus; when illegal immigrants risk their anonymity by demonstrating in public for their rights. But I distrust the idea that any one thing is 'constitutive' of politics, and disagree with both Arendt and Rancière when they try to bind us to one way

---

[60] Schaap 'Enacting the right to have rights', 35. He is commenting here on Jacques Rancière 'Who is the subject of the Rights of Man?' in Rancière *Dissensus: On Politics and Aesthetics* (London and New York: Continuum, 2010), 62–75.

of understanding equality, politics, or the human.[61] In some instances we establish our mutual equality through a political community; in others, we enact our equality against a community that denies it; this is the sense in which the human is both claim *and* commitment. It is, following Arendt, an expression of the commitment made by the members of a political community to recognise one another as equals. It is also, following Rancière, the enactment of equality against the odds, against the consensus, by those not currently regarded as members. Sometimes one, sometimes the other, sometimes one leading to the other. The key question is not whether there is an existing community or an explosion of dissensus; the crucial point is that equality is enacted as claim and commitment, and that the human is a political matter.

The capacity to think of oneself as an equal became more generally available – along with the capacity to see others as our equals – at particular periods of history (and I have no quarrel with the argument that 'narratives of suffering' played a role in this). Explanations are not, however, the same as justifications, and equality is not a matter of justification. Attempting to deduce it from essential features we are said to share has been a hostage to fortune, for there were always some humans who appeared not to exhibit the relevant features, and some non-humans who looked considerably better qualified. Making the essential features ever thinner and more abstract has not solved

[61] In 'Jacques Rancière and the problem of pure politics', Samuel Chambers makes a convincing case against the suggestion that Rancière has a 'pure' conception of politics, but I continue to think that Rancière sees dissensus as constitutive. *European Journal of Political Theory* 10 (2011), 303–26.

the problem, but introduced new ones in its place. When we assert our common humanity we are not justifying the right to be regarded as equal by reference to shared features; we are not even engaged in the quasi-justification that evokes solidarity by drawing attention to resemblances. The assertion of humanness is simultaneous with the assertion of equality.

4

Dignity and equality

We do not need substantive accounts of the human in order to justify treating one another as equals, nor – given the exclusionary risks attached – should we want such accounts. In this chapter, I address one key challenge to this position, which comes via the idea of human dignity. Dignity per se poses no problem for my argument. Nothing in what I have so far argued stops me valuing dignified behaviour, admiring the dignity of a Nelson Mandela, or advising a friend not to participate in an undignified slanging match. I may feel some ambivalence towards dignity, sometimes admiring it, sometimes wishing people would not stand so much upon it, but there is no inconsistency in me regarding dignity as a mostly desirable quality. Nor, indeed, is it incompatible with my arguments for me to regard dignified behaviour as to some extent species specific, to think that it would be odd to talk of ants as behaving in a dignified manner, though not especially strange to say this of cats. My problem arises when we start talking more specifically of 'the dignity of the human'. At this point we seem to be indicating some substantive ideal of what it is to be human, and what therefore counts as diminishing or degrading that humanness. Many consider this 'dignity of the human' a necessary underpinning for claims about human rights, but there is no good reason why the commitment to human equality should have to be underpinned in this way, nor why it should have to come as a second stage. Most of what people find useful in ideas about human dignity can be adequately provided for by going straight to equality instead.

The 'dignity of man' (sic) has figured as one of the bases for claiming rights for centuries, but it was mainly with the Universal Declaration of Human Rights in 1948 that the 'inviolable' dignity of the human became such a central reference point for human rights documents and legislation. It arguably came to play this role because of the difficulties of otherwise getting agreement on the nature of human rights. The signatories to the Declaration came from very different directions: they were Catholics and communists; came from East and West, North and South; they included some who attached primary importance to the individual and individual autonomy and others for whom we are always rooted in social relations and best viewed as part of a collective. There was little chance that this disparate group could arrive at a shared understanding of human rights, but they could all, it seems, agree on the importance of human dignity. As Christopher McCrudden puts it, 'a theory of human rights was a necessary starting point for the enterprise ... Dignity was included in that part of any discussion or text where the absence of a theory of human rights would have been embarrassing.'[1] This does not, he stresses, mean there was therefore a consensus on what human dignity meant, just that everyone thought it mattered.

The preamble to the Declaration puts it thus: 'Whereas recognition of the inherent dignity and of the equal and

[1] Christopher McCrudden, 'Human dignity and the judicial interpretation of human rights', *The European Journal of International Law* 19/4 (2008), 655–724: 678.

inalienable rights of all members of the human family is the foundation of freedom, justice and peace in the world...'
This does not represent inherent dignity as the foundation for human rights – the preamble puts them side by side as joint foundations for freedom, justice, and peace – but it is notable that it is dignity that is now claimed as inherent, not (as would have been more common in the natural law tradition) the rights themselves. In some of the subsequent legal uses, dignity does little work: it becomes a way of expressing the idea of human rights, so not so much a *basis* for those rights as another way of describing them. But there are also thicker versions, where dignity is seen 'as expressing a value unique to itself, on which human rights are built'.[2] In his review of the judicial interpretations of human rights documents – interpretations which involve adjudicating conflicts of rights or determining which has priority – McCrudden concludes that the thicker version has become the more prevalent. Dignity then emerges as the metaprinciple.

The importance of dignity in legal theory and judicial practice has been accompanied in recent years by an explosion of interest among political theorists. In 2012, Michael Rosen published *Dignity*, based on the Benedict Lectures at Boston University, and Jeremy Waldron published *Dignity, Rank, and Rights*, based on the Tanner Lectures at Berkeley. In 2011, George Kateb published a book on *Human Dignity*.[3] All three argue that we cannot talk of human rights without in some way

[2] McCrudden, 'Human dignity and the judicial interpretation', 680–1.
[3] Michael Rosen, *Dignity: Its History and Meaning* (Cambridge MA and London: Harvard University Press, 2012); Jeremy Waldron, *Dignity, Rank, and Rights* edited and introduced by Meir Dan-Cohen (Oxford University

referring to human dignity. Kateb goes furthest. He claims that we cannot defend human rights without in some way endorsing a philosophical anthropology: without identifying, that is, the uniquely human characteristics we seek to protect through our notion of human rights. This is a direct challenge to the points I have made so far.

Three arguments for human dignity

There are three main arguments for a notion of human dignity. (1) It is said to provide the grounding for human rights (question: why do we need rights? answer: so as to protect human dignity). (2) It enables us to explain and express the harm of degrading, humiliating, and contemptuous treatment. (3) It provides us with a way of identifying what is problematic in practices that the participants claim to be happy with and to which they have given their full consent. I have least to say about the first of these. It should be clear from what I have already argued that I do not set much store by the need to ground rights, or equality, or many of the other values we hold dear. We have to argue for them, for sure, and in doing so will draw on a range of argumentative strategies, including trying to convince people that if they do not endorse these particular rights or values they are being inconsistent with other values they hold dear, or arousing – in Richard Rorty style – their sympathies by describing what it is like to be deprived of these rights. It is implausible, however, that there might be some

Press, 2012); George Kateb, *Human Dignity* (Cambridge MA and London: Belknap Press of Harvard, 2011).

knock-down argument that takes the form of demonstrating that rights derive from a deeper 'thing': dignity. This is not how the complex psychology of winning people over works. The more fundamental objection is that grounding rights and equality in the inherent dignity of the human turns them into things we deserve *because* of our inherent dignity as humans. The implication, as I see it, is that we would no longer deserve the equality of treatment if we lacked this thing called dignity. But equality is not, and should not be regarded as, a matter of desert; it is not something we can come to deserve or to which we can lose our entitlement. On this point the American Declaration of Independence and French Declaration of the Rights of Man and Citizen have it right: equality is a starting point, not a second-stage deduction.

The potentially more powerful second argument is that human dignity gives us a language in which to express the harms of degrading, humiliating, and contemptuous treatment that cannot be captured by reference to pain alone. It simply isn't true that 'while sticks and stones may break my bones, words can never harm me'; and the kind of humiliation that is visited on offenders when they are required to cut off their hair or wear clothing that marks them out as criminals does not disappear when they are reminded that the hair will grow again or that the clothing is perfectly warm. Pain, suffering, and death are not the only harms we can do to people. There may be no lasting physical scars when a prisoner is made to crawl on his hands and knees with a dog collar round his neck, but in being treated like an animal he is being scorned, humiliated, and – we very commonly say – deprived of his human dignity. Given a choice, the prisoner might prefer this treatment to a savage beating. If he is of a particularly robust disposition, he might even escape the experience without lasting psychological scars. We do not normally see this as relevant. Humiliation matters; and being subject to degrading treatment is a harm even if, at the end of the process, you emerge entirely whole in body and mind.

The dehumanisation associated with this kind of treatment is sometimes a precursor to more directly physical harms, for in treating people as other than or less than human we close off that sense of a common humanity that might otherwise make us hesitate before attacking or killing them. It might then be argued that it is not the attack on human dignity that matters, but that this paves the way to actual physical attack. In his account of his time in Auschwitz, Primo Levi argues that the camps were organised in such a way as to destroy the prisoners' humanity. He describes the use of numbers instead of names, the shaved heads, the grotesque and never fitting clothing, the impossibility of keeping clean, the 'bestial' competition for food, all the ways in which the prisoners were made less than human, often in their own estimation as well. He writes of 'the resolution of others to annihilate us first as men in order to kill us more slowly afterwards'.[4] Descriptions of the 1994 genocide in Rwanda capture a similar process of dehumanisation as a prior condition for the killing: the widespread use of the term cockroaches to describe the Tutsis; the killers who said (this is a quote from a killer interviewed after the events) 'we no longer

---

[4] Primo Levi, *If This is a Man* (London: Abacus, 1987), 57 (first published 1958).

saw a human being when we turned up a Tutsi in the swamps'.[5] Those of more consequentialist bent might then argue that the harm of humiliating, contemptuous, dehumanising treatment lies precisely in its effects: so either in the psychological scars of the victim, or in paving the way to them being tortured and killed. Those who deploy the language of human dignity find this unconvincing, and so do I. Even when military discipline protects despised prisoners from physical harm (it sometimes does), or their own inner resilience enables them to shrug off a humiliating experience, being treated as less than or other than human is a harm in itself. We often describe it as an affront to human dignity.

But should we? While agreeing that there is an unacceptable humiliation, *not* reducible to physical or even psychological pain, we might still want to say it is the coercion – the exercise of tyrannical power forcing people to adopt postures they themselves regard as humiliating – that makes it unacceptable, not the activity itself. We humiliate when we make people occupy lesser – more humble – positions; we degrade when we force them into a lower grade; we express our contempt when we treat them as less worthy than ourselves. As the very language indicates, all these refer to states of inequality, to exercises of power that have positioned others as less worthy than oneself. The same points apply when we consider what is at stake in hospital patients being deprived of their dignity when they are left to lie in soiled linen, abandoned semi-naked on a hospital trolley, or talked at as if they were children. We can call these

[5] Cited in Stone, 'The Holocaust and "The Human"', 241.

'affronts to human dignity' if we so choose, but the crucial point is that people are being infantilised, treated as lesser beings, not treated as equals. We do not need a substantive account of what constitutes treating someone in the manner appropriate to human dignity in order to criticise this treatment. All we need is that patients are being treated in ways that the doctors and nurses would refuse to accept for themselves.

The third argument for human dignity is that it provides a way of identifying what is problematic in practices that the participants claim to be happy with and to which they have given their full consent. In the more Kantian versions of this there is a dignity in humanity that requires us to treat people as ends in themselves, not as things or mere means, and this duty extends not only to how we must treat others, but to how we should treat ourselves. There are certain things, that is, that are incompatible with human dignity, and it is not up to us to determine which these are. As a recent judgment from the German Constitutional Court puts it: 'human dignity means not only the individual dignity of the person but the dignity of man as a species. Dignity is therefore not at the disposal of the individual.'[6]

This last argument has proved particularly controversial, for when dignity is represented as 'not at the disposal of the individual', this suggests that societies are justified in banning practices that fully agentic and well-informed individuals have chosen to engage in. Some of the most robust contemporary denunciations of dignity – 'dignity is a useless

[6] Cited in McCrudden, 'Human dignity and the judicial interpretation', 705.

concept',[7] 'the stupidity of dignity'[8] – come from figures in the field of bioethics, a field informed by the view that what matters is full and informed consent, but also shaped by claims about human dignity. In the bioethical debates about the legitimacy of markets in body tissues, for example, Roger Brownsword identifies three broad positions. There is a utilitarian perspective that employs overall benefits to human welfare as the central criterion by which to judge whether such markets are desirable (and usually concludes that they are); there is a human rights view that insists on our right to control the uses made of our bodies and body products (and usually criticises the exploitation of our body tissues by the large biotechnology companies); and there is what he terms the 'dignitarian' view that considers any trade in body tissues as at odds with human dignity.[9] The critics of dignity are particularly incensed by the last. They argue that nebulous notions of human dignity are being inappropriately deployed to block fully consensual experiments and procedures.

This is not my objection – I am closer on this point to the dignitarians than to those who think that consent settles

[7] Ruth Macklin, 'Dignity is a useless concept', *British Medical Journal* 327 (2003), 1419–20.

[8] Steven Pinker, 'The stupidity of dignity', *The New Republic*, 28 May 2008.

[9] Roger Brownsword, 'Property in human tissue: triangulating the issue', pp. 93–104 in M. Steinmann, P. Sykora, and U. Wiesing (eds.) *Altruism Reconsidered: Exploring New Approaches to Property in Human Tissue* (Farnham: Ashgate, 2009). We find a similar divide in arguments about markets in live human organs, the uses of in vitro technology to create saviour siblings, or to enable commercial surrogacy. For further discussion of this, see my book *Our Bodies, Whose Property* (Princeton University Press, 2013).

all – but I will argue that this too is better understood as a matter of equality. Dignity relies on a normatively loaded, sometimes quasi-religious, almost inevitably substantive understanding of what it is to be human. It also makes our entitlement to equal respect depend on hierarchical claims about us being better, or more valuable, than other species. As I argue in the next chapter, I do not support a thoroughgoing project of 'decentring the human' of the kind proclaimed in some of the writings on posthumanism. But while we cannot simply dislodge humans from the centre of our moral and political universe, we should also avoid endorsing a moral hierarchy that dwells on us as superior beings. Dignity is problematically substantive, and problematically hierarchical as well.

Dignity, autonomy, equality

Critics of dignity have made much of what they see as the indeterminacy in notions of dignity, the capacious way it gets deployed on opposing sides of an argument (on both sides, for example, of the debates over euthanasia), and the contradiction in saying that human life has inalienable dignity and that torture is wrong because it takes that dignity away. Most of these objections can be adequately met by differentiating a bit more carefully between the various meanings and uses of dignity,[10] and I do not regard any of these points as definitive. I focus here on the relationship between dignity, autonomy, and

[10] As, for example, in Doris Schroeder, 'Dignity: two riddles and four concepts', *Cambridge Quarterly of Healthcare Ethics* 17 (2008), 230–8; Suzy Killmister, 'Dignity: not such a useless concept', *Journal of Medical Ethics* 36, (2010), 160–4. Alasdair Cochrane argues against dignity, but also

equality, and how these are addressed in recent political theory. Is it important, as proponents of human dignity argue, to be able to claim certain ways of behaving as at odds with human dignity, even when those engaging in them do not find them such? Can something be an affront to human dignity even when we do not personally think it so?

Though Michael Rosen ultimately defends a notion of human dignity, he queries some of the more substantive accounts and makes a strong case for our 'right to behave in an undignified way'.[11] He is concerned that when governments take it on themselves to determine what is an affront to human dignity (one might think here of the German Constitutional Court telling us that dignity is not at the disposal of the individual), they may take this as a license to ban what they view as *undignified*, and thereby restrict the scope for irreverent behaviour. He tells an appealing story about the good uses to which undignified behaviour was put in the opening of Haggerston Baths in London in 1904, where the first part of the ceremony was dominated by the usual (no doubt rather pompous) speeches from municipal dignitaries, but the climax came when Alderman Wakeling took the first plunge into the pool 'surprising everyone' (to quote the local paper) 'by swimming under water the full length of the bath'.[12]

This is not an especially challenging case of undignified behaviour, and seems to refer to what is sometimes described as

usefully disambiguates the various meanings of the term: 'Undignified bioethics', *Bioethics*, 24/5 (2010), 234–41.

[11] Rosen, *Dignity*, 70.

[12] *Hackney and Kingsland Gazette* June 27, 204, quoted in Rosen, 72.

'comportment dignity'[13] rather than the more loaded notion of 'species dignity'. But Rosen also engages with the more arresting case, widely cited in the literature of dignity, when the mayor of a French municipality banned a dwarf-tossing competition on the grounds that the practice was at odds with human dignity. Manuel Wackenheim, the dwarf in question, responded that it was the ban that violated his dignity by preventing him from taking up the employment of his choice, and launched an ultimately unsuccessful legal appeal. Rosen regards the dwarf-tossing case as a good example of the elision of dignity with 'dignified behaviour'. Dwarf-tossing, he says, is undoubtedly undignified; it may even be that when some dwarves freely sign up for the activity they thereby contribute to a lowering of the esteem in which the wider community of dwarves is held. 'But being esteemed less because one happens to be associated in others' minds with the behavior of someone who behaves in an undignified way? I'm sorry, but in my view people just have to put up with it.'[14]

Jeremy Waldron is more willing than Rosen to employ substantive accounts of dignity. Drawing on the extensive uses of the notion in contemporary jurisprudence, but also on the very practice of law itself, he stresses the way law represents us to ourselves as rights bearers capable of standing up for those rights, and he pulls out of this the continuing salience of notions of noble bearing, self-possession, walking upright, walking tall, as important elements in the contemporary understanding of

---

[13] In Schroeder, 'Dignity: two riddles and four concepts'; and Killmister, 'Dignity: not such a useless concept'.

[14] Rosen, *Dignity*, 70.

human dignity. He is well aware that these link back to an explicitly non-egalitarian – or, rather, pre-egalitarian – discourse in which dignities were attached to hierarchically arranged stations and only those of highish rank could claim to walk tall. He argues, however, that 'the modern notion of *human* dignity involves an upwards equalization of rank, so that we now try to accord to every human being something of the dignity, rank and expectation of respect that was formerly accorded to nobility.'[15]

James Whitman's analysis of the way forms of punishment that used to be highly differentiated between high- and low-status prisoners were subsequently equalised upwards provides a neat illustration of this. In eighteenth-century France, high-status prisoners – who were often political prisoners – were treated in very different ways to 'common criminals', and were allowed to serve out their punishment in relatively dignified surroundings. In the course of Voltaire's several periods of imprisonment in the Bastille, for example, he was allowed access to books, writing materials, and visitors; and though he was arrested because of his supposedly seditious writings, he was nonetheless able to get on with writing some more. In his case, there was never any likelihood that he would have to endure the forced labour or frequent physical beatings that were the common lot of low-status prisoners. Over the subsequent centuries, Whitman argues, the more favourable – more respectful – treatment meted out to high-status prisoners was generalised: 'more and more offenders have been subjected to the relatively respectful treatment that was the privilege of a

---

[15] Waldron, *Dignity, Rank, and Rights*, 33.

tiny stratum of high status persons of the eighteenth century'.[16] (Countries that did not differentiate to the same extent between high- and low-status prisoners – his key example is the USA – also did not, he argues, go through this levelling-up process, hence his otherwise rather paradoxical claim that the country that was more egalitarian in its beginnings has ended up as the one with the harsher punishment regime.)

Waldron argues that this kind of levelling up has been part of a wider pattern, such that we are now said to owe to everyone the kind of respect that used to be reserved for those of high rank. As historical analysis, this looks entirely plausible. What concerns me is the suggestion that what it now means to be human, and therefore deserving of this respect, is being able to walk tall, walk proud, and hold oneself up high. This suggests an objective standard of dignified human behaviour. That objective standard looks, moreover, distinctly gendered: 'walking tall' versus bending to the needs of others; 'walking proud' versus meekness and docility; there is a strong gender coding here. In this account, human dignity invokes a substantive understanding of what it is to be human that is skewed towards certain types of human and certain types of human behaviour. It lends itself to the kinds of criticism I have already made regarding substantive understandings of the human.

As regards the dwarf-tossing case, Waldron does not finally commit himself, but stresses that 'an analysis in terms of

[16] James Q. Whitman, *Harsh Justice: Criminal Punishment and the Widening Divide Between America and Europe* (Oxford University Press, 2005), 10.

autonomy would be quite different from an analysis in terms of dignity',[17] and indeed represents this as one of the reasons why notions of human dignity are so important. If we were to assess the dwarf-tossing case entirely in terms of autonomy, we would limit ourselves to questions about whether the dwarf knew what he was getting himself into and freely agreed to the terms of the contract, and would be left with little more to say if all the autonomy requirements had been met. Were we to analyse the issues, however, in terms of dignity, this would at least leave open the possibility that there are further considerations. A concern for human dignity might require us to ban certain practices even when fully agentic individuals can be shown to have consented to them.

For George Kateb, meanwhile, it is almost the whole point of human dignity that it allows us to identify harms that involve what he terms 'painless oppression', harms that we may not recognise as such, perhaps because we have been brain-washed, or simply because we are not yet sufficiently attuned to the requirements of human dignity.[18] He offers, as illustration, the inhabitants of Aldous Huxley's *Brave New World*.[19] There is a clear hierarchy of human beings in the Brave New World and life is hard for the lower ones. But for the Alphas and Betas, at least, life 'After Ford' is good: there is no war, no fear of death, plenty of recreational sex, readily available

---

[17] Waldron, *Dignity, Rank, and Rights*, 141.

[18] Kateb, *Human Dignity*, 20.

[19] This novel is widely cited in discussions of dignity; it figures also in Francis Fukuyama's *Posthuman Future* and Leo Kass, *Life, Liberty and the Defense of Dignity: The Challenge for Bioethics* (San Francisco: Encounter Books, 2002).

hallucinogenic drugs, and minds perfectly adjusted to the life they are leading through a steady stream of conditioning messages. If we nonetheless think (as Huxley clearly intends us to) that these lives are lacking – that the inhabitants of the Brave New World are diminished, perhaps even dehumanised, by their dependence on banal messages of comfort or regular doses of soma – we seem to be invoking some notion of human dignity. It is irrelevant that most of the inhabitants are entirely at ease with the life, or that they regard Bernard Marx, the not quite hero, as a weirdo because he prefers to dispense with the drugs and – as he puts it – 'be himself'. Even if everyone in the Brave New World insisted on their satisfaction with their lot, and no one experienced even the vaguest of longings for a different kind of life, we might still want to say these people are living lives that are not fully human. Yet as Kateb notes, 'there is no deliberately inflicted pain, or any remediable pain or suffering that is neglected by the authorities'. In his analysis, 'It is human dignity that is violated.'[20]

For its advocates, then, human dignity enables us to identify harm in practices that leave neither physical or psychological scars, that people claim to be happy with, and to which they have given their full consent. On this point, it stands in direct opposition to a libertarian principle that views us as self-owners, and therefore free – subject to the standard provisos about not blocking anyone else's freedom – to do what we like with our bodies and lives. From the self-ownership perspective, if I do not consider it beneath me to sell my services in a dwarf-tossing competition, become a sex-worker, sell a spare kidney,

---

[20] Kateb, *Human Dignity*, 84.

or live a life of mindless banality, who are you to say it is? If I do not feel my dignity compromised, or simply don't care that much about dignity, it would be outrageous, on this view, for any government to try to stop me.

Outrageous, but of course what many governments do. Most countries ban markets in live human organs and often explicitly invoke notions of human dignity when they do so; very many ban prostitution; and though Manuel Wackenheim contested the dwarf-tossing ban right up to France's Conseil d'Etat, and even appealed to the UN Human Rights Committee, he was not able to reverse it. The devotee of self-ownership would position herself very much on his side: would say it is for each of us to decide what, if anything, conflicts with our dignity, and not a matter for the paternalistic state. This is not my position – I am no fan of self-ownership[21] – but I agree with at least this aspect of the libertarian position: that there are problems in setting up human dignity as something entirely independent of what we (subjectively) feel it to be. One person might have an especially elevated notion of human dignity: might think, with Kant, that it is at odds with human dignity for people to sell their hair. Another might have a less robust understanding: might quite plausibly say that if she doesn't feel her dignity threatened, it is inappropriate for anyone else to say that it is. The point is not that people disagree about normative issues. This is something we learn to live with, and given that we learn through disagreement, is no bad thing. The point about human dignity is that it implies something independent

---

[21] For my objections to self-ownership, see Phillips, *Our Bodies, Whose Property?*

of what you or I feel to be dignified – some standard beyond our subjective ones, grounded in a thesis about what it is, essentially, to be human. While I agree with dignitarians that there is more at stake in many issues than whether we have given our full and informed consent, I find it more helpful to address these without recourse to the notion of dignity.

Consider, in this context, the sex trade. There is considerable pain, suffering, and coercion in the sex trade, hence some relatively 'easy' grounds on which one might criticise and regulate it. But not all sex workers are the abused and trafficked victims of deception. Some, at least, enter the business with full knowledge of what they are doing and actively choose it over other ways of making a living; some even manage to get personal satisfaction from the work. If we want, nonetheless, to say there is something problematic about sex work (I do), it looks as if we have to call on something like human dignity: something that allows us to regard selling sex for money as a lessening of human dignity or status even when the participants do not find it such. I do not, however, want to say this. I do not want to say that people are degraded, demeaned, or diminished by signing up as sex workers. My instincts, if anything, lead in the opposite direction: towards the view that we must start from what people themselves articulate about feeling insulted, humiliated, or degraded, and not indulge in claims about false consciousness. While agreeing therefore with what I take to be the core of the notion of human dignity – that pain and suffering are not the only harms we can do to people, and that consenting to something does not stop it being harmful – I believe we can adequately address this through ideas of human equality.

Equality not dignity

In *What Money Can't Buy*, Michael Sandel argues that there are two grounds on which one might object to a particular kind of market.[22] We might say that certain transactions are unfair (he does not use this term, but let's call them exploitative), either because of the kind of trickery and deception that bedevils the sex trade, or because background inequalities in bargaining position effectively coerce people into agreeing to something that is deeply unfair. The dwarves might say they are 'happy' to be tossed around in a competition as if they are no more than bundles of clothing, but what they mean by this may be that they find it impossible to get work because of their unusual stature, or impossible to get other kinds of work that are sufficiently well paid. The lap dancers might thoroughly dislike their work – would never agree to do it if they had a 'real' choice – but they may be desperate to finance the university degree that will enable them to move on to something else. The objections here would be on the grounds of agency: that what seems like consent is not really so once we take into account the inequality in background conditions. There is a second objection, however, that might come into play even if all the autonomy conditions were met: in Sandel's arguments, this 'focuses on the character of the goods themselves and the norms that should govern them'.[23] He argues that the commodification of some goods (sex, kidneys, children) is problematic because it involves treating these 'according to a lower mode of

---

[22] Michael Sandel, *What Money Can't Buy: The Moral Limits of Markets* (New York and London: Allen Lane, 2012).

[23] Sandel, *What Money Can't Buy*, 113.

valuation than is appropriate' to them.[24] Their nature is diminished, degraded, or demeaned when they are made available for sale. I take this to be very much the kind of argument that underpins notions of human dignity.

I share with Sandel the view that there is more at stake in assessing events and activities than whether participants freely consent to them and, like him, believe that even contracts fairly entered into can be problematic. But I see this more in the terms set out by Carole Pateman many years ago in *The Sexual Contract*: not as an argument about it being at odds with human dignity to trade in certain kinds of goods, but as a point about even contracts freely and fairly entered into still being, in some contexts, contracts of inequality and subordination.[25] An agreement to sell (sex, kidneys, children) can be at odds with equality, not only because it is hard to see why people would agree to it in the absence of background inequalities, but because if they do agree – for whatever reasons – the contract they have entered into involves one human being subordinated to the power and authority of another.

We ban markets in slaves and children at least partly on this ground, and while many employ the language of human dignity to explain why we ban them, the crucial point is that these markets involve some humans assuming total authority over the lives and futures of others. This is incompatible with a commitment to human equality. It is my view (I have argued this elsewhere[26]) that prostitution, however freely

---

[24] Sandel, *What Money Can't Buy*, 33.

[25] Carole Pateman, *The Sexual Contract* (Cambridge: Polity Press, 1988).

[26] Phillips, *Our Bodies, Whose Property?*

entered into, similarly renders the bodies of some people subject to the authority of others. The authority, in this case, is
not total – this is part of the reason why we do not simply ban
markets in sex in the same ways as we ban markets in slaves or
children – but the power relationship inherent in the arrange-
ment still undermines claims about all humans being equal.
Markets in live human organs, however freely entered into by
agents who know what they are doing and have the option
to act otherwise, similarly render the bodies of some people
into sources of spare parts for the bodies of others, in ways
that undermine the commitment to human equality. It is not
just that some people thereby become means for others rather
than ends in themselves: I tend to agree with the critics who
argue that the distinction between treating others as ends-in-
themselves and treating them merely as means does not hugely
help, for cases where people are treated *only* as means are rare,
and cases where we treat people badly do not always involve
treating them as means.[27] The more straightforward objection
in the case of markets in live human organs is that these position buyer and seller as unequals. Whether the inequality then
constitutes enough of a case for banning the market is a more
complex question: for myself, I do not support a ban on the
sex trade, but strongly support maintaining the current almost
universal ban on the trade in human organs. Like Waldron in his
comments on the dwarf-tossing case, however, I want to insist

---

[27] As Alasdair Cochrane puts it, it would be impermissible to keep a
plumber locked up in my shed so he can be available to fix my radiators
whenever I need him, to treat him, that is, exclusively as a means, 'but
keeping him in my shed and never making use of his plumbing skills
would be equally impermissible'. 'Undignified bioethics', 238.

that important questions remain even when all autonomy conditions have been met. Choice does not legitimate everything, and the free choice of individuals in agreeing to a particular exchange should not be our only moral touchstone.[28]

I also want to insist that framing this in terms of dignity adds little, and that in many of its formulations human dignity simply *is* human equality. Denise Réaume argues that 'valuing human dignity means acknowledging the inherent worth of human beings; therefore violating dignity involves conveying the message that some are of lesser worth than others'.[29] What is this other than a statement that humans are to be regarded as equals? The prohibition on degrading or humiliating treatment is, in essence, a prohibition on exercises of power that represent some people as of lesser worth than others. The idea that people need a basic minimum of resources to live a life of human dignity is, in essence, an equality right; it says that all humans need enough to live on, not just the more privileged ones. Even the privacy uses of dignity language – in legal judgments regarding abortion or homosexuality – revolve around the idea that it is at odds with human dignity (to my mind, read human equality) for the power to take these important decisions to reside in someone other than those most immediately concerned.

---

[28] This is strongly argued in Heather Widdows, 'Rejecting the choice paradigm: Rethinking the ethical framework in prostitution and egg sale debates', pp. 157–80 in Sumi Madhok, Anne Phillips, and Kalpana Wilson (eds.) *Gender, Agency and Coercion* (Basingstoke: Palgrave Macmillan, 2013).

[29] Denise G. Réaume, 'Discrimination and dignity', *Louisiana Law Review* 63, (2003), 645–95: 672.

Consider Waldron's account of the meaning of dignity:

> Dignity is the status of a person predicated on the fact that she is recognised as having the ability to control and regulate her actions in accordance with her own apprehension of norms and reasons that apply to her; it assumes she is capable of giving and entitled to give an account of herself (and of the way in which she is regulating her actions and organising her life), an account that others are able to pay attention to; and it means finally that she has the wherewithal to demand that her agency and her presence among us as a human being be taken seriously and accommodated in the lives of others, in others' attitudes and actions towards her, and in social life generally.[30]

In my reading of this, dignity is here being used to refer to equality of status. It refers to being recognised as an agent 'capable of giving and entitled to give an account of herself', not therefore to be pushed around and spoken for by others; to being able to insist that one's agency and presence are taken seriously and not, I presume, just taken 'seriously' (which might not commit us to very much) but taken as seriously by those others as their own. So why not just say equality? Consider, in similar vein, Whitman's account of the importance now attached to dignity in the German criminal justice system, as evidenced in prisoners being able to wear their own clothes, being addressed in a respectful manner, and offered work in 'real' jobs that approximate conditions in the workplace outside. His gloss on this, again, sounds to me like equality: 'The lives of convicts are

[30] Jeremy Waldron, 'How law protects dignity', *The Cambridge Law Journal* 71/1 (2012), 200–22: 202.

supposed to be, as far as possible, no different from the lives of ordinary German people. Convicts are not to be thought of as persons of a different and lower status than everybody else.'[31] So why not just say equality? Dignity is often just another way of describing what it is to treat others as our equals. When it isn't – when it edges into problematically substantive notions of what it is to be human – it edges into something we would do better to avoid.

Dignity as hierarchy

In his reply to critics in *Dignity, Rank, and Rights*, Waldron observes that 'many of the moral philosophers I talk to about dignity begin by being quite sceptical about whether there is work for the concept to do that isn't already being done by other concepts (for example, value, autonomy, or respect). Their impulse seems to be that we should get by with as few normative concepts as possible – as though concepts were expensive.'[32] He is right, of course; asking why we need a notion of dignity, or what is 'added' by it, implies unnecessary parsimony in relation to concepts. This is a salutary warning. There is no reason in principle why we cannot talk about dignity *and* respect *and* equality; no reason, also, why these should not overlap in their meanings and sometimes refer to the same thing.

There is also a salutary warning contained in Rosen's account of the anti-egalitarian associations of dignity in nineteenth-century Catholic teaching, where the predominant idea was that 'all members of society have dignity, but their

[31] Whitman, *Harsh Justice*, 8.   [32] Waldron, *Dignity, Rank, and Rights*, 135.

dignity consists in their playing the role that is appropriate to their station'.[33] Hence the highly suspect 'dignity of labour' or 'dignity of motherhood'. Claiming the dignity of labour has certainly mattered to otherwise undervalued manual workers, and claiming the dignity of motherhood has mattered to otherwise undervalued mothers, but dignity still functions here as camouflage rather than any sustained challenge to inequality. The crucial meaning conveyed is that 'X has dignity, therefore does not need equality'. Meanwhile, the 'dignity of life' continues to block consideration of the well-being of women faced with unwanted or dangerous pregnancies leading, in the tragic case of Savita Halappanavar in Ireland, to the death of the woman because the doctors would not terminate even an unviable foetus. Rosen comments that the way dignity has figured in that Catholic tradition may explain 'why so many egalitarians I know who have had a Catholic education are allergic to the concept of dignity'.[34] As an egalitarian who was brought up Catholic, I take his point.

I do not, however, accept that my arguments reflect only personal history or excessive parsimony about concepts, and my allergy to notions of human dignity is strengthened by the frequent insistence on it as *high* rank. In George Kateb's formulation, 'All individuals are equal; no other species is equal to humanity. These are the two basic propositions that make up the concept of human dignity.'[35] 'The core idea of human dignity is that on earth, humanity is the greatest type of beings.'[36]

[33] Rosen, *Dignity*, 49.
[34] Rosen, 'Dignity past and present', in Waldron, *Dignity, Rank, and Rights*, 88.
[35] Kateb, *Human Dignity*, 6.   [36] Kateb, *Human Dignity*, 3.

The human species 'is the only animal species that is not only animal, the only species that is partly not natural'.[37] Kateb claims that there is no species snobbery in this, and since he later unpacks the uniqueness of humans as including our crucial role as stewards of nature – the only species, he says, that 'can perform the three indispensable tasks: keep the record of nature, understand nature, and appreciate it'[38] – he clearly is not claiming us as the only species that matters nor saying that we can do as we wish with the others. There is still something troubling about this repeated emphasis on our high value and superiority.

I do not take the view that animals have the same rights as humans. I do not even take the modified version associated with the Great Ape Project, which calls for some of the rights commonly granted to human animals – to life, for example, the protection of individual liberty, and protection against torture – to be extended to chimpanzees, gorillas, and orangutans.[39] This is not, I hasten to add, because I think we should feel free to torture chimpanzees. My position reflects, rather, the arguments made in the preceding chapters, where I challenge the notion that our claim to be treated as equals or recognised as having various human rights is grounded in our possession of some essential human characteristics, and the implication that if other animals also exhibit these characteristics they too qualify for some of that same consideration. Whatever treatment we owe to other animals, it is no more grounded in their

[37] Kateb, *Human Dignity*, 11.

[38] Kateb, *Human Dignity*, 114.

[39] Paola Cavalieri and Peter Singer (eds.) *The Great Ape Project: Equality Beyond Humanity* (London: Fourth Estate Publishing, 1993).

possession of certain supposedly 'human' characteristics than is the treatment we owe to other humans; and when we accord rights to other animals it is not because they turn out to be half human. My objection to Kateb is not that he discriminates between human and non-human animals. It is that he makes so much of our *superiority*.

5

Humanism and posthumanism

In my opening comments, I indicated that I did not intend this book as either an endorsement of humanism or an anti- or posthumanism. What do I mean by this claim? Peter Sloterdijk says of humanism that 'as a word and as a movement [it] always has a goal, a purpose, a rationale: it is the commitment to save men from barbarism'.[1] His description nicely captures the association between humanism and the humanities, linking it back to the 'civilising' scholarship of the Renaissance and its Greek and Roman forebears. It also captures some of humanism's political naivety: its belief that good men and good books can save us from the abyss. That naivety remains one of the charges against humanism, though many of today's critics read this in a more sinister light, variously identifying humanism's hypocrisy, anthropocentrism, Westerncentrism, exaggerated confidence in scientific progress, and misguided belief that humans can (eventually) control their world. My own preoccupation is that, in steering us away from the particularities that shape and define us – and through which we shape and define ourselves – humanism renders these of lesser significance, and thereby makes it harder to address the power relations invested in them. My objection then reflects a longstanding

---

[1] Peter Sloterdijk, 'Rules for the Human Zoo: a response to the Letter on Humanism', *Environment and Planning D: Society and Space* 27 (2009), 12–28: 15.

commitment to conceptualising equality *through* rather than *despite* difference. As applied to humanism, this becomes a concern that diverting attention from difference to what, as humans, we have in common can encourage an empty sentimentalism that wishes away the realities of power. This is a harsh depiction, and no self-defined humanist would recognise herself in the description, but it is hard to see how humanism can entirely avoid the charge. The force of the tradition lies precisely in that movement away from what is seen as an excessive and destructive focus on the differences that divide us, and towards our common humanity: this movement is the very basis of its ethical appeal. Humanism seeks to awaken us to commonality as more important than difference, and it does this through the abstraction of the human.

That abstraction is only slightly lessened when we stress (as a number of contemporary theorists now do; as I have done myself in some recent writing[2]) the vulnerable body as what unites us. When the human is figured as rational will, the abstraction is self-evident and the scope for exclusion is wide. Focusing by contrast on the body promises a more secure basis for commonality. Bodies, surely, are less abstract than minds, more grounded in daily reality; and while bodies have, historically, been ranked according to their presumed ability to feel pain, the body is, in principle, less open to exclusionary hierarchies than a humanness – or personhood – defined through cognitive capacities. There is evidence that people find it harder to treat others as less than human when forced to engage with

---

[2] In both Phillips, *Multiculturalism without Culture* and *Our Bodies, Whose Property?*

them as embodied beings, as when past participants in genocidal killings describe the moment of eye contact with the person they are about to destroy and their realisation, in that moment, that they are not killing a cockroach or subhuman being but a fellow human.[3] As Dan Stone puts it in a discussion of testimony from the Rwanda massacres, 'recognizing the humanity of the victim is disastrous for the self-assurance of the genocidal killer'.[4] These fragile moments of recognising oneself in the other are typically physical in their nature. It is things like seeing someone stoop in a way that reminds you of your father, or being forced to look an enemy in the eye, that confront you with a common humanity.

Bodies matter; and mentally erasing them is one of the ways we erase our commonality. And yet 'the body' is in many ways as abstract as 'the mind', and whatever we may tell ourselves about all bodies sharing the same needs and experiencing the same vulnerabilities, that never seems to stop us differentiating between the ones whose needs we care about and the others. The body is sometimes what enables us to see beyond the stereotypes and suspicions to a shared humanity. But it is also what produces the almost visceral disgust that sustains racism, misogyny, homophobia, and so many hatreds of the other; and failing to register this double dynamic can lead to the sentimentalism with which humanism is often charged. Judith Butler is one of those whose recent work has focused on the precariousness of life and vulnerability of the body, and she

---

[3] Dan Stone gives examples of this from the Rwandan conflict in 'The Holocaust and "The Human"'.

[4] Stone, 'The Holocaust and "The Human"', 241.

represents this as potentially enabling us to see one another as equals: that, at least, is how I understand her comment that 'the recognition of shared precariousness introduces strong normative commitments of equality'.[5] This has laid her open, however, to criticism for moving from a political to a more exclusively ethical register. In Bonnie Honig's reading, for example, Butler now gives us a 'universal humanist ethics of lamentation in which the focus is on suffering,'[6] the worry being that this edges too close to a transcendence of politics, to the invocation of a shared mortality that will enable us to get beyond otherwise intractable political divisions. In an argument that has some overlap with my own, Honig wants to resist moves that make our common humanity depend on an ability to see beyond those political divisions; in her argument, simply substituting the vulnerable body for the rational mind does not 'save' humanism.

Humanism remains problematic, even when detached from its more cerebral versions and re-framed around the body. *Anti*-humanism, however, is hardly an attractive location (as the old joke against Louis Althusser used to put it: 'when I hear the word human I reach for my gun'), and Butler is by no means alone in working towards a position that more closely approximates the humanist tradition than its starker opposite. A recent book by Sonia Kruks draws on Simone de Beauvoir to argue for a 'humanism after posthumanism', and sees the

---

[5] Judith Butler, *Frames of War: When is Life Grievable?* (New York and London: Verso, 2009), 28–9.

[6] Bonnie Honig, *Antigone, Interrupted* (Cambridge University Press, 2013), 42.

distinctiveness of de Beauvoir's (non-abstract) humanism as reflecting the significance she attaches to embodiment.[7] Nikolas Kompridis draws on Jacques Derrida to argue that 'we can no longer afford the luxury of knee-jerk anti-essentialism or unreflective anti-humanism'; in his argument, too, there is an emphasis on embodied corporeality, or more specifically 'intercorporeality', as a way of thinking about what it means to be human.[8] Despite her critique of mortalist humanism, even Bonnie Honig is willing to describe her own position as a humanism, so long as it is prefaced by the qualifier 'agonistic' and engages 'themes of *thumos*, pleasure and eroticism, not just hunger, loss and death'.[9]

Posthumanism 1: the continuing critique of humanism

If humanism has its difficulties, and anti-humanism too readily dismisses what remain key values, what then of posthumanism? There are three key ways in which posthumanism has come to figure in recent literature: as a continuing critique of humanism that drops the starker anti-humanist overtones; as an anticipation of a future populated by enhanced or hybrid humans; and as an unsettling of the boundaries between human, animal, and machine. Rosi Braidotti's *The Posthuman* is a good illustration of the first. She adopts the

---

[7] Sonia Kruks, *Simone de Beauvoir and the Politics of Ambiguity* (Oxford University Press, 2012), ch. 1.

[8] Nikolas Kompridis, 'Technology's challenge to democracy: what of the human?', *Parrhesia* 8 (2009), 20–33: 23.

[9] Honig, *Antigone, Interrupted*, 193.

label to mark her continued distance from humanism – which she sees as anthropocentric, Westerncentric, and projecting an image of human perfectibility in terms of autonomy and self-determination – but also her growing reluctance to jettison key humanist ideals of freedom and emancipation.[10] In this move, posthumanism becomes the preferred self-description because both humanism and anti-humanism are problematic. It then shares the weakness of many 'post' claims: a tendency to render what is being superseded in over-simplistic terms, producing its own superiority by the way it writes up the past, but also claiming any significant reformulation of the earlier tradition as necessarily *post* humanist. In Braidotti's case, this produces some odd co-options. Edward Said, who was pretty explicit about his project of developing a humanism without its colonial taint, is described as engaged in a 'posthuman quest';[11] while Seyla Benhabib's work on cosmopolitanism (which I cannot for a moment think she would describe as posthuman) is said to 'resonate positively with [Braidotti's] situated posthuman ethics'.[12]

In general, both the earlier anti-humanism and this more recent posthumanism tend to represent humanism in terms that few of its advocates would accept. (I appreciate that I may also be doing this in my worries about the obliteration of

[10] Rosi Braidotti, *The Posthuman* (Cambridge: Polity Press, 2013).

[11] Braidotti, *The Posthuman*, 47. This is at odds with Said's own comments in 'Orientalism, 25 years on' (2003) where he says 'I have called what I try to do "humanism", a word I continue to use stubbornly despite the scornful dismissal of the term by sophisticated post-modern critics.' Reprinted in Barry F. Seidman and Neil J. Murphy (eds.) *Towards a New Political Humanism* (Amherst, NY: Prometheus Books, 2004).

[12] Braidotti, *The Posthuman*, 53.

difference.) In one representative account – this is taken from Neil Badmington, but I could have chosen many other sources – humanism is described as 'a discourse which claims that the figure of "Man" (sic) naturally stands at the centre of things; is entirely distinct from animals, machines and other nonhuman entities; is absolutely known and knowable to "himself"; is the origin of meaning and history; and shares with all other human beings a universal essence.'[13] If this is indeed what humanism entails, its critics are surely right to protest: 'naturally stands', 'entirely distinct', 'absolutely known and knowable', 'the origin of meaning and history', and so on. But who exactly thinks this? Stark oppositions between a defunct humanism and superior posthumanism are neither useful nor convincing, and one reflection of this is that many of those cited as inspirations for posthumanism refuse the name. Donna Haraway, for example, is endlessly cited in the literature on posthumanism with reference to her 1985 'Manifesto for cyborgs', but does not herself endorse the term. She dislikes the hubris often associated with pronouncements about posthumanism, the way people get caught up in ever more exaggerated science fiction fantasies, the way they forget, in the process, how many unsolved problems remain as regards being human. As she puts it, 'I never wanted to be posthuman, or posthumanist, any more than I wanted to be postfeminist.'[14]

[13] Neil Badmington, 'Mapping posthumanism', *Environment and Planning A* 36 (2004), 1344–51: 1345. To be fair to Badmington, he explicitly argues against notions of supersession or radical break, so his description here is somewhat at odds with his general argument.

[14] Donna J Haraway, *When Species Meet* (Minneapolis and London: University of Minnesota Press, 2008), 17. Her 'Manifesto for cyborgs:

Posthumanism 2: posthuman, transhuman, superhuman beings

The second version of posthumanism is almost a humanism run wild, at least if one accepts the representation of humanism as celebrating the human capacity to master the natural world. The precise focus varies, depending on whether exponents are primarily steeped in the world of cybernetics and robotics or that of gene enhancement. The former anticipate a future in which the distinction between intelligent human and intelligent machine becomes more or less irrelevant. In Katherine Hayles' (critical) depiction, 'the posthuman view privileges informational pattern over material instantiation' and 'configures the human being so that it can be seamlessly articulated with intelligent machines'.[15] The human body then becomes the rather archaic housing of what really matters, which is the capacity to compute and think. Science fiction often projects a future populated by robots that look disturbingly like us: the kind of scenario conjured up by Philip K. Dick, for example, in the book that inspired the film *Bladerunner*, where robots so perfectly simulate and anticipate humans that they can only be identified by highly trained personnel testing their capacity for empathy and affect. (Empathy is still thought to be the one thing robots don't get.) Those working in the field of

science, technology and sociality-feminism in the 1980s' was first published in *Socialist Review* 80 (1985), 65–108.

[15] N. Katherine Hayles, *How We Became Posthuman: Virtual Bodies in Cybernetics, Literature, and Informatics* (University of Chicago Press, 1999), 2–3.

artificial intelligence or robotics rarely share this preoccupation with the human form, and are more likely to get excited by the possibilities of downloading human consciousness into a computer and creating a human/machine hybrid.[16] When processing information becomes the essential defining activity, the material in which this takes place – organic body, mechanical device, hybrid of the two – becomes largely incidental.

For those extrapolating from genetic research, by contrast, the posthuman condition is envisaged as involving creatures who continue to look like us, but have much enhanced capacities. In this projected future, scientists have the capacity to identify, modify, and remove problematic genes, and can not only eradicate genetically transmitted disease through the pre-implantation diagnosis of embryonic material, but can manipulate genetic material to achieve a more fundamental reshaping of the human. 'Ultimately,' writes Nick Bostrom, 'it is possible that such enhancements may make us, or our descendants, "posthuman", beings who may have indefinite health-spans, much greater intellectual faculties that any current human being – and perhaps entirely new sensibilities or modalities – as well as the ability to control their own emotions.'[17] In this

---

[16] Hayles cites Hans Moravec in *Mind Children: The Future of Robot and Human Intelligence* (Harvard University Press, 1988) as an example of the erasure of the human body. As she puts it, 'when information loses its body, equating humans and computers is especially easy, for the materiality in which the thinking mind is instantiated appears incidental to its essential nature.' Hayles, *How We Became Posthuman*, 2.

[17] Nick Bostrom, 'In Defense of Posthuman Dignity' *Bioethics* 19/3, 2005: 202–214 at p. 203. He uses the term 'posthuman condition' to refer to

scenario, we hold on to our bodies – though the identification of emotional control as a major gain of enhancement suggests a similar imagining of the posthuman as the moment when we free ourselves from the constraints of our bodily natures - and become more exclusively 'mind'.[18]

Much of this remains in the realm of science fiction. Single genes do not typically correlate with single propensities, and the idea that we could eliminate the chances of people succumbing to depression or make them brilliant at maths by manipulating the genome is a pretty distant extrapolation. It is not, however, entirely far-fetched.

Political and ethical debate has mostly focused on the issues raised by this second scenario of human enhancement, which is said to fundamentally change human nature, threaten human dignity, undermine human autonomy, and destroy the basis for human rights. In what I have argued so far, I have

circumstances where at least one of the following holds: 'Population greater than 1 trillion persons; Life expectancy greater than five hundred years; Large fraction of the population has cognitive capacities more than two standard deviations above the current human maximum; Near-complete control over the sensory input, for the majority of people for most of the time; Human psychological suffering becoming rare occurrence; Any change of magnitude or profundity comparable to that of one of the above.' Nick Bostrom, 'The future of humanity', in Jan-Kyrre Berg Olsen, Evan Selinger, and Soren Riis (eds.) *New Waves in Philosophy of Technology* (New York: Palgrave McMillan, 2009), 63–4. (One hopes the first two in particular don't happen simultaneously!).

[18] As argued in Samuel Wilson and Nick Haslam, 'Is the future more or less Human? Differing views of humanness in the posthumanism debate', *Journal for the Theory of Social Behaviour* 39/2 (2009), 247–66. See also Kompridis, 'Technology's challenge to democracy'.

criticised accounts of the human that specify essential defining features, and accounts of human dignity that invoke substantive characteristics. Neither of these is therefore my own preferred line of attack. The 'natural' in human nature is almost impossible to identify, if by natural we mean existing outside social relations; and being 'natural' has no obvious normative significance, since what comes naturally can be bad as well as good. When we talk of human nature we selectively endorse certain characteristics as more important to us than others, and our assessments of what counts as 'changing human nature' will then reflect these judgements rather than matters of fact.[19] As for human dignity, if we take this to mean anything other than that humans are equal, the concept is more likely to benefit the supporters of human enhancement than its detractors. When Bostrom, for example, challenges the view that enhancement threatens human dignity, he selects an explicitly non-egalitarian reading of dignity: 'Dignity as a Quality', 'being worthy, noble, honourable',[20] dignity as 'composure' and 'self-contained serenity'.[21] Having laid out what he sees as the substantive qualities attached to dignity, he then quite plausibly argues that enhanced (trans)humans could be far more

[19] Norman Daniels observes that we are unlikely to think that making everyone three inches taller than before is 'changing human nature'; but might well think we had changed human nature if we eliminated the capacity for emotion. 'Can anyone really be talking about ethically modifying human nature?' pp. 25–42 in Julian Savulescu and Nick Bostrom (eds.) *Human Enhancement* (Oxford University Press, 2009), 33–35.

[20] Nick Bostrom, 'Dignity and enhancement', *Contemporary Readings in Law and Social Justice* 84 (2009), 84–115: 86.

[21] Bostrom, 'Dignity and enhancement', 88.

dignified in their behaviour and bearing than the rest of us.[22] If we take dignity as referring to substantive characteristics, it is hard to make a compelling case about human enhancement threatening it. It is only when we recognise dignity as another way of saying equality that any such case becomes compelling.

The standard bioconservative arguments about human enhancement undermining human nature and destroying human dignity do not convince. Since we do not need a theory of human nature in order to ground human rights, the claim that enhancement destroys the basis for human rights is similarly unconvincing. Jürgen Habermas offers an alternative line of critique, drawing on the language of freedom and self-determination, but this too misses what I see as the central point.[23] Habermas' key objection to the engineering of human life – which he frames as parents creating what they believe to be 'better' children – is that this restricts the freedom to live a life of one's own. It means the children discover themselves as 'products' of an engineering process. This will be problematic, he argues, even if the engineering proves unsuccessful and people make of themselves something very different to the plan,

---

[22] The form of his argument reveals dignity not just as non-egalitarian, but positively anti-egalitarian: 'let us pause and ask ourselves just how much Dignity as a Quality a person has who spends four or five hours every day watching television . . . Who has never had an original idea, never willingly deviated from the path of least resistance, and never devoted himself seriously to any pursuit or occupation that was not handed him on the platter of cultural expectations?' Bostrom, 'Dignity and enhancement', 99.

[23] Jurgen Habermas, *The Future of Human Nature* (Cambridge: Polity Press, 2003).

for whatever the outcome, the engineering represents an 'invasion' into the very 'core of a future person'.[24] Habermas notes that enhancement also offends against equality, creating an inequality between the parents who can indeed live a life of their own, and their children who are denied this possibility; but he has little to say about the more pressing inequalities threatened between the now favoured superbeings and the rest. I take it that this is because he does not see being a 'superbeing' – a trans- or posthuman – as a desirable condition. The bigger worry, to me, is what these dreams of the post- or transhuman do to our ideas of human equality.

It is already the case that inequalities of wealth in one generation translate into inequalities of wealth in the next, not just through the direct transmission of inherited wealth, but through the capacity to purchase superior health and education for one's children and to mobilise one's contacts to secure their career success. At present, we can rely on some minor counter-movements to this, through social policy interventions, but also through the recalcitrance of individuals who sometimes achieve extraordinary things despite the least propitious of circumstances, or prove immune to parental prodding and engage in downward social mobility. Yet imagine a world in which wealth's capacity to purchase the most promising environments combined with the capacity to purchase the most promising genetic make-up: here there would be virtually no space left for countervailing movements. In his 1958 meritocratic dystopia, Michael Young delivered a biting critique of a society that measures worth exclusively by performance in

[24] Habermas, *The Future of Human Nature*, 87.

intelligence tests.[25] One of the central points in that critique was that if intelligence (or rather, being good at IQ tests) displaced everything else as the sole principle of social organisation, there would be no counter-hierarchies in which you might be a failure at one thing but a success at another. In the old society, those at the bottom of the social hierarchy could always console themselves with the belief that they were in some ways better than their social superiors. They could think that if they had only had the same chances, they too would have risen to positions of great influence and esteem. Meanwhile, those at the top of the hierarchy could never fully convince themselves that they had deserved their position, for they would always stumble across some individuals in lesser positions whose intelligence and abilities dwarfed their own. In a society organised exclusively on the basis of merit, however, the successful would be full of confidence that they did indeed deserve their position, while the unsuccessful would be left to face the unpalatable truth that they were objectively inferior. Subjective and objective status would then coincide. The point of Young's critique was not that we should therefore celebrate the older inequalities of opportunity. The point, rather, was that societies need to recognise and promote the plurality of virtues and talents, not reduce everything to one narrowly conceived 'intelligence', and not label everyone without that narrowly conceived intelligence as a failure.

In Young's dystopia, everything is concentrated into one dimension. In the dystopia celebrated in writings on the

[25] Michael Young, *The Rise of the Meritocracy, 1870–2033: An Essay on Education and Equality* (London: Thames and Hudson, 1958).

trans- or posthuman there is a similar kind of concentration. Those with money are able to buy not only the better environment, but the better genes, the intelligence-enhancing drugs, the replacement tissue and organs as required. Those without are stuck in the 'merely human' mould. Those with least money of all might end up – as some already do – as the sources of the life-saving replacement tissue and organs for the more privileged. Francis Fukuyama challenges the posthuman nightmare as fundamentally changing human nature. Habermas challenges it as fundamentally restricting human freedom. I see it as at odds with the equality I take to be the core message of 'the human'. When we invoke notions of the human, we are engaged in establishing ourselves as equals. We are making both a claim and a commitment to view often very different others as equal to ourselves. This is not about recognising an already existing equality, and does not depend on being able to 'prove' shared features of human beings; it does not, in that sense, depend on empirical evidence. The ability, however, to think all humans as equals *did* depend on certain historical conditions, and while there is a kind of ratchet effect at work with ideas like equality, we should not assume too readily that things cannot go into reverse. Under radically altered conditions, the capacity to make that commitment could be radically undermined.

There is a line of argument that brushes aside egalitarian concerns about the prospects for human enhancement by pointing to the many existing ways in which people already enhance their own or future children's life prospects and the many existing inequalities we seem to live quite happily with; and then represents the inequalities associated with human enhancement as simply a development of these.[26] This says, in effect, that none of these inequalities – current or future – threatens the fundamental commitment to seeing all humans as equal; that 'equality' and inequalities can live happily side by side. But the toleration of actual inequalities has more of an impact on ideas of human equality than this suggests, for it becomes increasingly difficult to hold on to even the formal acknowledgement of equality when people live substantially different lives. We see this already in the UK (without the aid of human enhancement) in the contemptuous treatment of people living on welfare benefits: no one yet proposes to remove their basic civil and political rights, but some of the ways of referring to the poor or those living on 'sink' estates do begin to suggest a species apart.[27] We also see it in the USA, in the treatment meted out to convicted prisoners who are, of course, often deprived of their voting rights even after completing their sentences and are subjected, while prisoners, to humiliations that seem to deny their shared humanity.[28] The commitment to

---

[26] Bostrom, for one, sees nothing especially new in the inequalities associated with technological enhancement: 'Modern, peaceful societies can have large numbers of people with diminished physical or mental capacities along with many other people who may be exceptionally physically strong or healthy or intellectually talented in various ways. Adding people with technologically enhanced capacities to this already broad distribution of ability would not need to rip society apart or trigger genocide or enslavement. 'In defense of posthuman dignity', 207.

[27] Owen Jones, *Chavs: The Demonization of the Working Class* (London: Verso, 2011).

[28] James Whitman argues that 'On the deepest level, American criminal justice displays a resistance to considering the very personhood of offenders'. Whitman, *Harsh Justice*, 9.

equality is not grounded in, or proven by, actual equality; but (contra Arendt) the capacity to make and sustain that commitment does depend on certain enabling material conditions.[29] We risk moving into an era where those enabling conditions disappear.

I am not claiming any 'genocidal potential' in human enhancement: that the genetically enhanced will feel themselves entitled to enslave the 'standard-issue humans', or that they will come to view them as beings that can be unproblematically destroyed.[30] But we do not need such doomsday scenarios to anticipate the erosion of our already fragile ideas of human equality. We need only consider the ease with which people have denied that equality in the past, and the many current discrepancies between a seemingly universal endorsement of ideas of human equality and the persistent denial of that idea in the ways peoples are treated.[31] We live in a historical moment when there is widespread genuflection before the ideal of equality – as before its political counterpart, democracy – while our

[29] See the arguments in Richard Wilkinson and Kate Pickett, *The Spirit Level: Why Equality is Better for Everyone* (London: Penguin Books, 2010).

[30] As argued in George Annas, 'The man on the moon, immortality and other millennial myths: the prospects and perils of human genetic engineering', *Emory Law Journal* 49/3 (2000), 753–82. This view is criticised in Eric T. Juengst, 'What's taxonomy got to do with it? "Species integrity", human rights and science policy', pp. 43–58 in Savulescu and Bostrom (eds.) *Human Enhancement.*

[31] Though he broadly defends human enhancement, Allen Buchanan acknowledges what he describes as an 'extremely serious' 'Practical Worry' that the enhanced could come to treat the unenhanced as their inferiors. 'Moral status and human enhancement', *Philosophy and Public Affairs* 37/4 (2009), 346–81: 371.

social and economic practices make this seeming commitment more and more of a hypocrisy. It is here that the real threat of the posthuman lies, and here that we so urgently need both national and international regulation.

Posthumanism 3: troubling the boundaries

The third body of posthuman literature (despite her refusal of the term, this would include Haraway) focuses on developments that unsettle the boundaries between human, animal, and machine. Those engaged in this do not talk the language of superhuman beings. To the contrary, they stress the continuities and mutual dependence between human and non-human. They talk of hybrids and cyborgs; point to robots that are not only immeasurably cleverer than us at calculation, but capable of generating new ideas;[32] note that swamp cabbages, humans, and beluga whales are all mostly made up of water;[33] endorse a 'vitalist materialism' that queries the division between organic and inorganic matter;[34] or delight, like Haraway, in 'the fact that human genomes can be found in only about 10 percent of all the cells that occupy the mundane space I call my body; the other 90 percent of the cells are filled with the genomes of bacteria, fungi, protists and such, some of which play in a symphony necessary to my being alive at all, and some of which are hitching a ride and doing the rest of

---

[32] N. Katherine Hayles, 'Computing the human', *Theory, Culture and Society* 22/1 (2005), 131–51.

[33] Astrida Neimanis, 'Feminist subjectivity, watered', *Feminist Review* 103 (2012), 23–41: 31.

[34] Jane Bennett, *Vibrant Matter: A Political Ecology of Things* (Durham and London: Duke University Press, 2010).

me, of us, no harm'.[35] The observations are meant to help us towards a more fluid and less anthropocentric understanding of our position in the world. The arguments sometimes refer to the developments in biotechnology, genetics, artificial intelligence, and nanotechnology that inspired celebrations of the post- or transhuman, but rather than imagining a future populated by amazing humans they use these to stress the increasingly anachronistic boundaries between humans and the rest. Mostly, moreover, these developments are said to enable us to see more clearly that the boundaries were always unsettled. We are encouraged to abandon notions of the human as uniquely differentiated from animals on the one side and machines on the other, to embrace the crossovers, co-existence, and uncertainties of where we end and others begin, and finally abandon the anthropocentrism that many see as characterising the humanist vision of the world.

The critique of anthropocentrism is not, of course, limited to posthumanism. Any work on animal rights challenges the view that humans are uniquely important, but may do this from explicitly humanist directions. Martha Nussbaum, for example, takes issue with those who think the sphere of justice applies only to humans. If we see justice as generated by contract, that restriction almost inevitably follows, for even in the most imaginative reconstruction it is hard to envisage human and non-human animals coming together to agree on a social contract. Against this, Nussbaum argues that we can derive animal entitlements from what it is for them to have a flourishing life, in much the same way as we can derive human entitlements

---

[35] Haraway, *When Species Meet*, 3–4.

from what humans need for a flourishing life.[36] This is an argument for justice to animals that draws on a broadly humanist understanding of what is necessary to human existence.
In *Zoopolis*, Sue Donaldson and Will Kymlicka challenge the
animal/human boundary to the point of proposing that we
regard (some) domesticated animals as co-citizens; again, the
case depends largely on extrapolation from arguments about
human capacities.[37] Animals – like humans – have interests,
preferences, and desires, and to varying degrees the capacity
to communicate these. And while even the most intelligent
of domesticated animals do not meet the highest conditions
for cognitive capacity (they cannot engage in deliberation, for
example), setting the conditions for citizenship at that level
would exclude large numbers of human beings. Drawing on
models of the way the cognitively disabled nonetheless exercise their agency through relationships with those they trust,
Donaldson and Kymlicka argue that domesticated animals can
also communicate, through their human companions, their
needs and concerns. As with Nussbaum's argument, this starts
from premises derived from the human, and uses these to challenge an anthropocentrism that considers animals as outside
the scope of justice. Neither of these could be said to argue a
posthuman position.

[36] Martha C. Nussbaum 'Beyond "compassion and humanity" Justice for
nonhuman animals' pp. 299–320 in Cass R. Sunstein and Martha C.
Nussbaum (eds.) *Animal Rights* (Oxford University Press, 2004);
Nussbaum *Frontiers of Justice* (Cambridge, MA: Harvard University
Press, 2006).
[37] Sue Donaldson and Will Kymlicka, *Zoopolis* (Oxford University Press,
2010).

A more plausible illustration is the work of Jane Bennett. Like Donna Haraway, Bennett does not embrace the term, but her argument about the vibrancy humans share with all kinds of organic and inorganic matter, and her insistence that we are not necessarily – or even mainly – the key actors in any series of events, edges closer to a posthumanism. (Bennett does not much care for labels, but notes that her work can be read as making '"posthumanist" gestures'.[38]) 'What would happen,' she asks, 'to our thinking about politics if we took more seriously the idea that technological and natural materialities were themselves actors alongside and within us – were vitalities, trajectories, and powers irreducible to the meanings, intentions or symbolic values humans invest in them?'[39] She gives one possible answer at the beginning of *Vibrant Matter*, when she expresses her hope 'that the story will enhance receptivity to the impersonal life that surrounds and infuses us, will generate a more subtle awareness of the complicated web of dissonant connections between bodies, and will enable wiser interventions into that ecology'.[40] She gives a further answer at the end, when she writes that 'encounters with lively matter can chasten my fantasies of human mastery, highlight the common materiality of all that is, expose a wider distribution of agency, and reshape the self and its interests'.[41]

---

[38] Bennett, *Vibrant Matter*, 120.

[39] Jane Bennett, 'A vitalist stopover on the way to a new materialism', pp. 47–69 in Diana Coole and Samantha Frost (eds.) *New Materialisms: Ontology, Agency, and Politics* (Durham and London: Duke University Press, 2010), 48.

[40] Bennett, *Vibrant Matter*, 4.   [41] Bennett, *Vibrant Matter*, 122.

In one of her more striking arguments, Bennett attributes 'thing-power' to a collection of rubbish she passes in the street, a collection that includes a dead rat, a plastic bottle cap, and a man's work glove. Stuff, she claims, is 'vital and alive in its own right', it has 'thing-power: it commands attention, exudes a kind of dignity, provokes poetry, or inspires fear', and she writes of the 'power' of the dead rat to 'make' her stop in her tracks.[42] We usually conceptualise this in terms of human agency: what 'makes' us stop in our tracks, we say, is not the rat, but the experiences and associations we humans attach to rats. Bennett calls on us to break out of that mind-set in which it is always us who set things in motion, always humans who give life or meaning to otherwise dead matter. Agency figures centrally in this: things act too, not in isolation, and not with intentionality, but act nonetheless in their ability to 'make a difference'.[43] Things happen through a crystallisation of many human and non-human elements, such that it becomes meaningless to identify specific humans as responsible for specific effects.[44] One of the benefits of this 'distributive theory of agency', she argues, is the attenuation of 'the blame game'.[45]

[42] Jane Bennett, 'The force of things: steps toward an ecology of matter', *Political Theory* 32/3 (2004), 347–72: 350.

[43] Bennett gives a particularly clear account of her understanding of things as 'actants' in Janell Watson, 'Eco-sensibilities: an interview with Jane Bennett' *Minnesota Review* 18 (2013), 147–58.

[44] A key example is the major power blackout in North America in 2003, which Bennett describes as 'the end point of a cascade – of voltage collapses, self-protective withdrawals from the grid, and human decisions and omissions'. *Vibrant Matter*, 25.

[45] Bennett, *Vibrant Matter*, 37.

In what she was working on prior to her death, Iris Marion Young also developed a critique of the backward-looking blame culture that focuses on attributing responsibility for past actions: the narrowly individualist 'liability' model that had come to dominate egalitarian political philosophy.[46] But the point, for Young, was to articulate an alternative, forward-looking, understanding of the responsibility individuals bear for structural injustice 'because they contribute by their actions to the processes that produce unjust outcomes'.[47] (Contributing, through our purchases of cheap clothing, to the appalling safety conditions in much of the garment industry in Bangladesh would be one clear example.) Like Bennett, Young proposed a distributive account of agency: instead of identifying levels of responsibility by tracing back specific outcomes to specific actions, we should come to see ourselves as responsible because of belonging with others in a system that delivers certain benefits and effects. In Young's account, however, it remains humans who are the agents, and humans who need to assume their responsibility for the systems in which they are enmeshed.

This is the point at which I diverge from the third strand of posthuman thinking. Dislodging us from our 'species-narcissism'[48] is a worthy objective. We would all benefit from more humility, and the respect for 'other critters' that one learns from reading Donna Haraway, or the 'eco-sensibility' one derives from reading Jane Bennett, are important counters to this narcissism. But we would also benefit – and here I return

[46] Iris Marion Young, *Global Challenges: War, Self-Determination and Responsibility for Justice* (Cambridge: Polity Press, 2007); *Responsibility for Justice* (Oxford University Press, 2011).

[47] Young, *Global Challenges*, 175.   [48] Bennett, 'A vitalist stopover', 59.

to some of Arendt's themes – from more responsibility, and that sets limits to how much we can decentre the human.[49] I do not mean, by responsibility, neo-liberal exhortations to get a grip, take responsibility for yourself, get on with your life: the individualised invocations of responsibility that ignore the unequal effects of social constraints. I mean, rather, that the sometimes overpowering weight of those constraints can encourage us to think there is nothing to be done; can encourage us, therefore, to abdicate our political responsibility. Arendt saw the denial of political responsibility – the opting out of politics, or the belief that things happened like forces of nature, or the abandonment of our own judgement in just agreeing to follow orders – as playing a large part in the rise of twentieth-century totalitarianism. While I do not endorse all the details of her analysis, I share these concerns. If we are troubled by hierarchies, we should warm to the critique of anthropocentrism. If we are additionally troubled by failures to act, we may worry about what gets lost in this.[50]

---

[49] In a similar argument, John Barry suggests that critiques of species-ism can reach a point where they conflict with moral responsibility: 'I contend that a naturalistic meta-ethical position turns on the idea that being human counts for something, concern with human interests is normatively significant, and that "speciesism" or prima facie favouritism towards members of one's own species is neither an "irrational bias", nor akin to sexism or racism as typically held by non-anthropocentric, ecocentric or deep ecological theorists. Rather, it is at the centre of any workable moral theory covering human-environmental interaction.' John Barry, 'Straw dogs, blind horses and post-humanism: The Greening of Gray?', *Critical Review of International Social and Political Philosophy* 9/2 (2006), 243–62: 245.

[50] I should stress that Jane Bennett isn't proposing we jettison all the significance we have attached to being human. 'To put it bluntly, my

It is also the case, that when it comes to the equality I have represented as at the heart of the notion of the human, there is no room for gradations. We cannot have a continuum in which some of the lesser humans sheer off into being 'more equal' to some of the greater animals, and we cannot have some humans more equal than others. Where equality is concerned, there is no getting away from the boundary dilemma: we are either in or out.

Since I began this book with a critique of the exclusionary uses of the human or person, this is a somewhat uncomfortable position to arrive at. Previous boundaries worked to exclude many people we now recognise as fully human: Native Americans, pygmies, women, indigenous Australians, to mention just those who have figured in earlier pages. In reflecting on that history, it seems reasonable to conclude that where we draw the boundary today may be as dubious as any of those earlier attempts. The category of the human has been deployed, historically, to draw a line and keep others out. If we no longer accept where many of the previous lines were drawn, why assume we have now got it right?

As someone who thinks all knowledge provisional, I cannot really fault this, but would stress again that the status of human is something we claim and enact rather than something we uncover. If humanness were grounded in a list of characteristics (capacity for agency, for example), then finding those characteristics in other beings – whether these were animals or

conatus will not let me "horizontalize" the world completely. I also identify with members of my species, insofar as they are bodies most similar to mine.' *Vibrant Matter*, 104.

things – would indeed put us in a quandary. We would either have to extend to them the category of human or stop attaching such overriding significance to the name. The linking of human with equality makes the second option unattractive. Since being human means being accepted as the equal of all other humans, it does indeed matter, and it is no wonder that people insist so much on it. Non-humans certainly have effects, but they are not going to demand to be regarded as humans – and if they did, that would be precisely when we should start rethinking the boundary.[51] I do not mean by this that no one gets accepted as human until they insist on it: there are plenty of humans who never think about claiming the name, the day-old baby for one. But whoever does claim to be human establishes themselves in that moment as an equal, and it is humans – not animals or machines – who do this.

Conclusion

My reservations regarding humanism, my rejection of posthumanism (2), and criticism of posthumanism (3), all revolve around their political effects. Let me end, then, by laying out once more what flows politically from my own understanding of the politics of the human. There are three main implications. First, rejecting a characteristics-based understanding of what it is to be human helps insulate us from the insidious

---

[51] Bennett discusses an exchange she had with Jacques Rancière, where she challenged him to say whether politics and democracy are necessarily about humans. Rancière's focus on equality, and the centrality of those moments when we constitute ourselves as equals, means that – like me – he does think this. Bennett, *Vibrant Matter*, ch. 7.

distinctions still widely made between different kinds of humans, on the grounds of their cognitive capacities, moral sensitivity, willingness to tolerate diversity, and so on. That people differ on these and many other scores is entirely irrelevant as regards their status as equals. So far as that status is concerned, being human is all that matters, and there are no gradations.

At the same time (this is the second implication), rejecting the abstract account of 'being human' as something separable from all the other identifiers of gender, race, ethnicity, culture, religion, nationality, sexuality, and so on, helps insulate us from a sentimental humanism – or a Christian benevolence – that stops short at the point of recognising us all as human. Though it is better than nothing when people set to one side the differences that had, up to that moment, made it hard for them to see one another as equals, the political challenge is to address the reasons why certain kinds of difference were ever conceived of as antithetical to equality. When recognising a shared humanity is treated as the end rather than beginning of the process, it operates like those early Catholic notions of human dignity, where being told that your way of life was replete with dignity became a coded way of saying you should therefore not bother your head with equality. We are not human *instead of* but *as* . . . women, men, black, white, gay, lesbian, heterosexual, and so on. In refusing the idea that these are alternative self-descriptions, the politics of the human pushes beyond an imagined equality towards strategies for tackling the (usually structural) causes of current inequality.

Finally, the claim-based account of what it is to be human moves the centre of attention away from those already

reasonably secure in their status as equals towards those still bat-
tling to achieve it. As one indication of the difference this might
make, consider again David Miller's account of the grounding of human rights. 'A theory of human rights,' he argues,
'must be able to explain why people in rich countries have
obligations of justice with respect to global poverty, or why
outsiders may have such obligations when a country is hit by
a natural disaster. It must be able to explain why humanitarian intervention may be justified to prevent governments or
other power-holders systematically violating the human rights
of their subjects. In other words, the theory of human rights
must identify moral claims that are powerful enough to impose
potentially demanding obligations on agents who are sometimes only loosely connected to the claimants themselves, and
also to override the sovereignty of established governments in
certain cases.'[52] In this formulation, the theory of human rights
is almost entirely addressed to those who already enjoy them: to
the people in rich countries, the outsiders, the agents of justice
rather than the claimants of rights.

The issues Miller addresses are important. People in
positions of power do have obligations, and working out what
these are – whether they are doing enough, but also whether
their belief in their obligations may have overstepped the
bounds – is a crucial political concern. Since the main reading public for political theory is people in richer countries and
richer people in poor countries, it is, moreover, hardly surprising that they should become the focus of attention. But

[52] David Miller, 'Grounding human rights', *Critical Review of International
Social and Political Philosophy* 15/4 (2012), 407–27: 410.

any exclusive focus on delineating these obligations limits the scope of both human rights and global justice, for these are ideas that come into their own when wielded by people denied their rights or deprived of justice. Every successive extension of rights to include wider categories of people has been helped by the humanitarian and campaigning activities of those already deemed human, but all extensions depend on the insistence of those previously excluded. Equality claimed has a greater force and more lasting impact than equality given, and it is here that the real radicalism of the politics of the human lies.

BIBLIOGRAPHY

Abu-Lughod, L. 'Writing against culture' pp. 137–62 in Richard G. Fox (ed.) *Recapturing Anthropology: Working in the Present* (Sante Fe, NM, School of American Research Press, 1991).

Agamben, G. *Homo Sacer: Sovereign Power and Bare Life* (Redwood City, CA, Stanford University Press, 1995).

Allen, D. 'Law's necessary forcefulness: Ralph Ellison and Hannah Arendt on the battle of Little Rock' in A. Smith Laden and D. Owen (eds.) *Multiculturalism and Political Theory* (Cambridge University Press, 2007).

Annas, G. 'The man on the moon, immortality and other millennial myths: the prospects and perils of human genetic engineering', *Emory Law Journal* 49/3 (2000): 753–82.

Althusser, L. *For Marx* (London, Penguin, 1969) first published 1966.

Anderson, K. *Race and the Crisis of Humanism* (London and New York, Routledge, 2007).

Arendt, H. 'On humanity in dark times: thoughts about Lessing' (1959) pp. 3–32 in Hannah Arendt *Men in Dark Times* (San Diego, CA and New York, Harcourt Brace, 1983).

 On Revolution (New York, Viking Press, 1963).

 'Reflections on Little Rock', *Dissent* Winter 1959: 45–56.

 The Human Condition (Chicago, IL, University of Chicago Press, 1958).

 The Origins of Totalitarianism (New York, Schocken Books, 1951).

Badmington, N. 'Mapping posthumanism', *Environment and Planning A* 36 2004: 1344–51.

Balibar, E. '(De)constructing the human as human institution: a reflection on the coherence of Hannah Arendt's practical philosophy', *Social Research* 74/3 2007: 727–38.

Barreto, J.-M. 'Rorty and human rights: contingency, emotions and how to defend human rights telling stories', *Utrecht Law Review* 7/2 2011: 93–112.

Barry, J. 'Straw dogs, blind horses and post-humanism: the greening of Gray?', *Critical Review of International Social and Political Philosophy* 9/2 2006: 243–62.

Benhabib, S. *The Rights of Others: Aliens, Residents, and Citizens* (Cambridge University Press, 2004).

Bennett, J. 'A vitalist stopover on the way to a new materialism' pp. 47–69 in Diana Coole and Samantha Frost (eds.) *New Materialisms: Ontology, Agency, and Politics.* (Durham, NH and London, Duke University Press, 2010).

'The force of things: steps toward an ecology of matter', *Political Theory* 32/3 2004: 347–72.

Vibrant Matter: A Political Ecology of Things (Durham, NH and London, Duke University Press, 2010).

Bohman, J. 'The moral costs of political pluralism: the dilemmas of equality and difference in Arendt's "Reflections on Little Rock,"' pp. 53–80 in L. May and J. Kohn (eds.) *Hannah Arendt: Twenty Years Later* (Cambridge, MA, MIT Press, 1996).

Bostrom, N. 'Dignity and enhancement', *Contemporary Readings in Law and Social Justice* 84 2009: 84–115.

'In defense of posthuman dignity', *Bioethics* 19/3 2005: 202–14.

'The future of Humanity,' pp. 186–215 in Jan-Kyrre Berg Olsen, Evan Selinger, and Soren Riis (eds.) *New Waves in Philosophy of Technology* (New York, Palgrave McMillan, 2009).

Bourke, J. *What it Means to be Human: Reflections from 1791 to the Present* (London, Virago, 2011).

Braidotti, R. *The Posthuman* (Cambridge, Polity Press, 2013).

Brownsword, R. 'Property in human tissue: triangulating the issue', pp. 93–104 in M. Steinmann, P. Sykora, and U. Wiesing (eds.) *Altruism Reconsidered: Exploring New Approaches to Property in Human Tissue* (Farnham, Ashgate, 2009).

Buchanan, A. 'Moral status and human enhancement', *Philosophy and Public Affairs* 37/4 2009: 346–81.

Butler, J. *Gender Trouble* (New York and Oxford, Routledge, 1990).

Frames of War: When is Life Grievable? (New York and London, Verso, 2009).

Undoing Gender (New York and London, Routledge, 2004).

Caney, S. *Justice Beyond Borders: A Global Political Theory* (Oxford University Press, 2005).

Canovan, M. *Hannah Arendt: A Reinterpretation of Her Political Thought* (Cambridge University Press, 1992).

Cavalieri, P. and Singer, P. (eds.) *The Great Ape Project: Equality Beyond Humanity* (London, Fourth Estate Publishing, 1993).

Chambers, S.A. 'Jacques Rancière and the problem of pure politics', *European Journal of Political Theory* 10 2011: 303–26.

Chouliaraki, L. *The Ironic Spectator: Solidarity in the Age of Post-Humanitarianism* (Cambridge, Polity Press, 2013).

Cochrane, A. 'From human rights to sentient rights', *Critical Review of International Social and Political Philosophy* 16/5 2013: 655–75.

'Undignified bioethics', *Bioethics* 24/5 2010: 234–41.

Cohen, G.A. 'Incentives, inequality and community,' pp. 331–98 in Stephen Darwall (ed.) *Equal Freedom* (Ann Arbor, University of Michigan Press, 1995).

'Where the action is: on the site of distributive justice', *Philosophy & Public Affairs* 26/1 1997: 3–30.

Daniels, N. 'Can anyone really be talking about ethically modifying human nature?' pp. 25–42 in Julian Savulescu and Nick Bostrom (eds.) *Human Enhancement* (Oxford University Press, 2009).

Dean, J. *Democracy and Other Neo-Liberal Fantasies: Communicative Capitalism and Left Politics* (Durham, NH and London, Duke University Press, 2009).

Dietz, M. 'Arendt and the holocaust' pp. 86–109 in Dana Villa (ed.) *The Cambridge Companion to Hannah Arendt* (Cambridge University Press, 2000).

Disch, L.J. 'On friendship in "Dark Times"' pp. 285–312 in Bonnie Honig (ed.) *Feminist Interpretations of Hannah Arendt* (Philadelphia, PA, Pennsylvania University Press, 1995).

Donaldson, S. and Kymlicka, W. *Zoopolis* (Oxford University Press, 2010).

Dossa, S. 'Human status and politics: Hannah Arendt on the Holocaust', *Canadian Journal of Political Science* 13/2 1980: 309–23.

Douzinas, C. *Human Rights and Empire: The Political Philosophy of Cosmopolitanism* (New York and London, Routledge, 2007).

Evans, E.P. *The Criminal Prosecution and Capital Punishment of Animals* (first published 1906, second edition London, Hesperus Press, 2013).

Ewald, W. 'Comparative jurisprudence (1): what was it like to try a rat?', *University Of Pennsylvania Law Review* 143/6 1995: 1889–2149.

Fassin, D. *Humanitarian Reason: A Moral History of the Present* (Oakland, CA, University of California Press, 2012).

Fernandez-Armesto, F. *So You Think You're Human?* (Oxford University Press, 2009).

Ferry, L.D.G. 'Floors without foundations: Ignatieff and Rorty on human rights', *Logos: A Journal of Catholic Thought and Culture* 10/1 2007: 80–105.

Foucault, M. *History of Sexuality Vol I* (New York, Pantheon Books, 1978).

The Order of Things (London, Tavistock Publications, 1970).

Franke, M.F.N. 'The unbearable rightfulness of being human: citizenship, displacement, and the right not to have rights', *Citizenship Studies* 15/1 2011: 39–45.

Fukuyama, F. *Our Posthuman Future: Consequences of the Biotechnology Revolution*, (New York, Farrar, Straus and Giroux, 2002).

Geras, N. *Solidarity in the Conversation of Humankind: The Ungroundable Liberalism of Richard Rorty* (London and New York, Verso, 1995).

Gilroy, P. *Against Race: Imagining Political Culture Beyond the Color Line* (Cambridge, MA, Belknap Press, 2000).

Goldin, C. and Rouse, C. 'Orchestrating impartiality: the impact of "blind" auditions on female musicians', *American Economic Review* 90/4 2000: 715–41.

Gray, J. *Straw Dogs: Thoughts on Humans and Other Animals* (London, Granta, 2002).

Griffin, J. *On Human Rights* (Oxford University Press, 2008).

Habermas, J. *The Future of Human Nature* (Cambridge, Polity Press, 2003).

Hacking, I. 'Making up people' in Thomas Heller, Morton Sosna, and David E. Wellbery (eds.) *Reconstructing Individualism: Autonomy, Individuality, and the Self in Western Thought* (Redwood City, CA, Stanford University Press, 1986).

Hanley, R.P. 'David Hume and the "Politics of Humanity"', *Political Theory* 39/2 2011: 205–33.

Haraway, D.J. 'Manifesto for cyborgs: science, technology and socialist-feminism in the 1980s', *Socialist Review* 80, 1985: 65–108.

When Species Meet (Minneapolis, MN and London, University of Minnesota Press, 2008).

Hayles, N.K. 'Computing the human', *Theory, Culture and Society* 22/1 2005: 131–51.

How We Became Posthuman: Virtual Bodies in Cybernetics, Literature, and Informatics (University of Chicago Press, 1999).

Heidegger, M. 'Letter on "Humanism"', first published 1946, reprinted pp. 239–76 in William McNeill (ed.) *Pathmarks* (Cambridge University Press, 1998).

Honig, B. *Antigone, Interrupted* (Cambridge University Press, 2013).

Hunt, L. *Inventing Human Rights: A History* (New York and London, WW Norton and Company, 2007).

James, S. 'Politics and the progress of sentiments' in Randall E. Auxier and Lewis Edwin Hahn (eds.) *The Philosophy of Richard Rorty* (Chicago and La Salle, IL, Open Court, 2010).

Jenkins, F. 'Sensate democracy and grievable life', in Moya Lloyd (ed.) *Butler and Ethics* (Edinburgh University Press, forthcoming 2015).

Jones, O. *Chavs: The Demonization of the Working Class* (London, Verso, 2011).

Kass, L. *Life, Liberty and the Defense of Dignity: The Challenge for Bioethics* (San Francisco, CA, Encounter Books, 2002).

Kateb, G. *Human Dignity* (Cambridge, MA and London, Belknap Press of Harvard, 2011).

Killmister, S. 'Dignity: not such a useless concept', *Journal of Medical Ethics* 36 2010: 160–64.

Kleingeld, P. 'Kant's second thoughts on race', *The Philosophical Quarterly* 57/229 2007: 573–92.

Kompridis, N. 'Technology's challenge to democracy: what of the human?', *Parrhesia* 8 2009: 20–33.

Kruks, S. *Simone de Beauvoir and the Politics of Ambiguity* (Oxford University Press, 2012).

Kukathas, C. 'Moral universalism and cultural difference' pp. 581–98 in John Dryzek, Bonnie Honig, and Anne Phillips (eds.) *Oxford Handbook of Political Theory* (Oxford University Press, 2006).

Juengst, E.T. 'What's taxonomy got to do with it? "Species integrity," human rights and science policy', pp. 43–58 in Julian Savulescu and Nick Bostrom (eds.) *Human Enhancement* (Oxford University Press, 2009).

Lacroix, J. 'The "right to have right" in French political philosophy: conceptualising a cosmopolitan citizenship with Arendt', forthcoming *Constellations*.

Laqueur, T.W. 'Bodies, details and the humanitarian narrative' pp. 176–204 in Lynn Hunt (ed.) *The New Cultural History* (Berkeley LA and London, University of California Press, 1989).

'Mourning, pity and the work of narrative in the making of "Humanity"' in Richard A. Wilson and Richard D. Brown (eds.) *Humanitarianism and Suffering* (Cambridge University Press, 2009).

Leigh, R.A. (ed.) *Correspondance Complète de Jean Jacques Rousseau*, Vol XXVII (Oxford, Voltaire Foundation, 1980).

Levi, P. *If this is a Man* (London, Abacus, 1987: first published 1958).

Macklin, R. 'Dignity is a useless concept', *British Medical Journal* 327 2003: 1419–20.

McCrudden, C. 'Human dignity and the judicial interpretation of human rights', *The European Journal of International Law* 19/4 2008: 655–724.

MacKinnon, C. *Are Women Human? And Other International Dialogues* (Cambridge, MA and London, Belknap Press of Harvard, 2007).

McMahan, J. 'Our fellow creatures', *The Journal of Ethics* 9 2005: 353–80.

Mann, N. 'The origins of humanism' in Jill Kraye (ed.) *The Cambridge Companion to Renaissance Humanism* (Cambridge University Press, 1996).

Menke, C. 'The "Aporias of Human Rights" and the "One Human Right": regarding the coherence of Hannah Arendt's argument', *Social Research* 74/3 2007: 737–62.

Miller, D. 'Grounding human rights', *Critical Review of International Social and Political Philosophy* 15/4 2012: 407–27.

National Responsibility and Global Justice (Oxford University Press, 2007)

Mills, C. 'Normative violence, vulnerability and responsibility', *Differences: A Journal of Feminist Cultural Studies* 18/2 2007: 157–79.

Moravec, H. *Mind Children: The Future of Robot and Human Intelligence* (Cambridge, MA, Harvard University Press, 1988).

Moyn, S. 'On the genealogy of morals' *The Nation*, April 16, 2007.

The Last Utopia: Human Rights in History (Cambridge, MA and London, Belknap Press of Harvard, 2010).

Murphy, A.V. 'Corporeal vulnerability and the new humanism', *Hypatia* 26/3 2011: 575–90.

Neimanis, A. 'Feminist subjectivity, watered', *Feminist Review* 103 2013: 23–41.

Nussbaum, M.C. 'Beyond "Compassion and Humanity" Justice for nonhuman animals', pp. 299–320 in Cass R. Sunstein and Martha C. Nussbuam (eds.) *Animal Rights* (Oxford University Press, 2004).

Frontiers of Justice (Cambridge, MA: Harvard University Press, 2006).

'Human functioning and social justice: in defense of Aristotleian essentialism', *Political Theory* 20/2 1992: 202–46.

Oberman, K. 'Beyond sectarianism? On David Miller's Theory of Human Rights', *Res Publica* 19/3 2013: 275–83.

Pateman, C. *The Sexual Contract* (Cambridge, Polity Press, 1988).

Peterson, V.S. and Parisi, L. 'Are women human? It's not an academic question' pp. 132–60 in Tony Evans (ed.) *Human Rights Fifty Years On: A Reappraisal* (Manchester University Press, 1998).

Phillips, A. 'Defending equality of outcome', *Journal of Political Philosophy* 12/1 2004: 1–19.

Gender and Culture (Cambridge, Polity Press, 2010).

Multiculturalism without Culture (Princeton University Press, 2007).

Our Bodies, Whose Property? (Princeton University Press, 2013).

Pinker, S. 'The stupidity of dignity', *The New Republic*, 28 May 2008.

Pitkin, H.F. *The Attack of the Blob: Hannah Arendt's Concept of the Social* (University of Chicago Press, 1998).

Puwar, N. *Space Invaders: Race, Gender and Bodies Out of Place* (London, Berg, 2004).

Rancière, J. 'Who is the subject of the Rights of Man?' pp. 62–75 in Rancière *Dissensus: On Politics and Aesthetics* (London and New York, Continuum, 2010).

Réaume, D.G. 'Discrimination and dignity', *Louisiana Law Review* 63 2003: 645–95.

Rorty, R. *Contingency, Irony and Solidarity* (Cambridge University Press, 1989).

'Human rights, rationality, and sentimentality' in Stephen Shute and Susan Hurley (eds.) *On Human Rights: The Oxford Amnesty Lectures* (New York, Basic Books, 1993).

'Reply to Susan James' in Randall E. Auxier and Lewis Edwin Hahn (eds.) *The Philosophy of Richard Rorty* (Chicago and La Salle, IL, Open Court, 2010).

'Response to Norman Geras' in Matthew Festenstein and Simon Thompson (eds.) *Richard Rorty: Critical Dialogues* (Cambridge, Polity Press, 2001).

Rosen, M. *Dignity: Its History and Meaning* (Cambridge, MA and London, Harvard University Press, 2012).

Ryan, A. *On Politics: A History of Political Thought from Herodotus to the Present* (London, Allen Lane, 2002).

Said, E. 'Orientalism, 25 years on', first published in 2003, reprinted in Barry F. Seidman and Neil J. Murphy (eds.) *Towards a New Political Humanism* (Amherst, Prometheus Books, 2004).

Sandel, M. *What Money Can't Buy: The Moral Limits of Markets* (New York, and London, Allen Lane, 2012).

Sartre, J.-P. *Anti-Semite and Jew: An Exploration of the Etiology of Hate* (New York, Schocken Books, 1948).

'Existentialism and humanism' (1945) reproduced as pp. 25–57 in Stephen Priest (ed.) *Jean-Paul Sartre: Basic Writings* (London and New York, Routledge, 2001).

'Preface' in Frantz Fanon *The Wretched of the Earth* (London, Penguin, 1967, first published 1961).

Scarry, E. 'The difficulty of imagining other persons' pp. 277–309 in Carla Hesse and Robert Post (eds.) *Human Rights in Political Transitions: Gettysburg to Bosnia* (New York, Zone Books, 1999).

Schaap, A. 'Enacting the right to have rights: Jacques Rancière's critique of Hannah Arendt', *European Journal of Political Theory* 10/1 2011, 22–45.

Schroeder, D. 'Dignity: two riddles and four concepts', *Cambridge Quarterly of Healthcare Ethics* 17 2008: 230–8.

Singer, P. *Animal Liberation* (New York, Avon, 1975).

Sloterdijk, P. 'Rules for the human zoo: a response to the letter on humanism', *Environment and Planning D: Society and Space* 27 2009: 12–28.

Stone, D. 'The Holocaust and "The Human"' pp. 232–49 in Richard H. King and Dan Stone (eds.) *Hannah Arendt and the Uses of History: Imperialism, Nation, Race and Genocide* (New York and Oxford, Berghahn Books, 2007).

Waldron, J. *Dignity, Rank, and Rights* Meir Dan-Cohen (ed.) (Oxford University Press, 2012).

'How law protects dignity', *The Cambridge Law Journal* 71/1 2012: 200–22.

Watson, J. 'Eco-sensibilities: an interview with Jane Bennett', *Minnesota Review* 18 2013: 147–58.

Whitman, J.Q. *Harsh Justice: Criminal Punishment and the Widening Divide Between America and Europe* (Oxford University Press, 2005).

Widdows, H. 'Rejecting the choice paradigm: rethinking the ethical framework in prostitution and egg sale debates' pp. 157–80 in Sumi Madhok, Anne Phillips and Kalpana Wilson (eds.) *Gender, Agency and Coercion* (Basingstoke, Palgrave Macmillan, 2013).

Wilkinson, R. and Pickett, K. *The Spirit Level: Why Equality is Better for Everyone* (London, Penguin Books, 2010).

Wilson, R.A. and Brown, R.D. (eds.) *Humanitarianism and Suffering* (Cambridge University Press, 2009).

Wilson, S. and Haslam, N. 'Is the future more or less human? Differing views of humanness in the posthumanism debate', *Journal for the Theory of Social Behaviour* 39/2 2009: 247–66.

Wollstonecraft, M. *A Vindication of the Rights of Woman: With Strictures on Political and Moral Subjects* (Boston, Peter Edes, 1792).

Young, I. M. *Global Challenges: War, Self-Determination and Responsibility for Justice* (Cambridge, Polity Press, 2007).

Justice and the Politics of Difference (Princeton University Press, 1990).

Responsibility for Justice (Oxford University Press, 2011).

INDEX